PHILIPPE LACOUE-LABARTHE'S

PHRASE

SUNY SERIES,
LITERATURE...IN THEORY

PHILIPPE LACOUE-LABARTHE'S

PHRASE

Infancy, Survival

CHRISTOPHER FYNSK

STATE UNIVERSITY OF NEW YORK PRESS

Published by State University of New York Press, Albany

Printed in the United States of America

For information, contact State University of New York Press, Albany, NY
www.sunypress.edu

Production, Laurie D. Searl
Marketing, Michael Campochiaro

Library of Congress Cataloging-in-Publication Data

Names: Fynsk, Christopher, 1952– author.
Title: Philippe Lacoue-Labarthe's *Phrase* : infancy, survival / Christopher Fynsk.
Description: Albany : State University of New York Press, 2017. | Series: SUNY series, literature . . . in theory | Includes bibliographical references and index.
Identifiers: LCCN 2016020986 (print) | LCCN 2016038965 (ebook) | ISBN 9781438463476 (hardcover : alk. paper) | ISBN 9781438463483 (pbk. : alk. paper) ISBN 9781438463490 (e-book)
Subjects: LCSH: Lacoue-Labarthe, Philippe. *Phrase.* | Lacoue-Labarthe, Philippe—Criticism and interpretation.
Classification: LCC PQ2672.A2417 Z49 2017 (print) | LCC PQ2672. A2417 (ebook) | DDC 848/.91407—dc23
LC record available at https://lccn.loc.gov/2016020986

10 9 8 7 6 5 4 3 2 1

CONTENTS

INTRODUCTION

The Throw of Infancy

In the course of a visit to Brooklyn in the winter of 2000, Philippe Lacoue-Labarthe presented me with a copy of *Phrase*, a book he had been composing for almost twenty-five years.[1] I answered this gesture on the same occasion by presenting him with a copy of *Infant Figures*, a text on which I had been working over a period in which he and I had not been in frequent contact—hence his surprise. But I would be no less surprised when I discovered, after extensive work with *Phrase*, just how singular a crossing this was.

Infant Figures was a book devoted, in its core section, to the *first*—not first principles, but first figurations, or, more precisely, primary figurations of an original exposure that haunts all conscious life.[2] Maurice Blanchot's portrayal of the death of the *infans* in *The Writing of the Disaster*, and Jacques Lacan's treatment of Freud's account of the dream of the "burning child" in *The Interpretation of Dreams*, offered platforms for a meditation on the structure and experience of this persisting exposure. The insistence of the motif of a dying in each of these scenes lent itself almost inevitably to an evocation of primal agonies, and thus to connections like those offered to a dream recounted by Primo Levi, to figures offered by Francis Bacon (which echoed, in their turn, words from Nietzsche on the topic of cruelty), and to other brutal or difficult images. The theme of the death of the *infans* cannot but evoke a register of painful associations—and this too was part of the book's burden: the many deaths of the innocent that remain with all of us. But the scene—hardly a "scene"—offered by Blanchot also gave witness to a joy and a release in that exposure, an "endless flow of tears," and then an enigmatic survival that Blanchot qualified as "living by acquiescence to the refusal, . . . waiting and watching."[3] That acquiescence, I suggested, would be the source of a latent relation on the order of an *opening*, a "yes" that would escape the hold of the negative, thus giving us the grounds for envisioning a relationality that would exceed not just the hold of any dialectic, but the power of the negative from which dialectic takes its movement. This opening would offer, for the one writing later, the possibility of *another relation* to alterity, and with this another thought of the ethical relation. The evidence of an originary need for figuration offers, at the same time, a vital perspective on the conditions and character of that writing.

For Philippe Lacoue-Labarthe, the thought of the primal exposure from which I proceeded in *Infant Figures* had been no less gripping, no less exigent. That we should have met there in our trajectories of writing should not ultimately have been so surprising, given what we had always shared in core attunements and our common engagement with the question of human finitude, a question opened crucially in the last century by Heidegger and then translated powerfully in modern French thought by a wide range of writers that included Blanchot and Lacan. Our common friendship with Jean-François Lyotard, who had taken up the topic of infancy in the late 1980s would also have prepared the way for this meeting. But the real extent of Lacoue-Labarthe's preoccupation with the question of infancy was not really visible until the publication of *Phrase*, this powerful piece of poetry, prose-poetry, dramatic writing, and reflection that he had drafted and repeatedly reworked over the course of more than two decades. The persistent publication (and even republication) of a few key sections from this work had hinted at the importance of the project for him.[4] But with the final publication of *Phrase* in book form, it became clear that it went to the core of Lacoue-Labarthe's efforts as a writer and thinker. Jean-Christophe Bailly, who came to this same conclusion, named it "the center around which everything turned."[5]

Circumstances relating to Lacoue-Labarthe's health in the last two decades of his life, and then his death in 2008, delayed my response to the book. I felt it required a reading no less searching and honest than Lacoue-Labarthe's efforts in composing it. Having lived in close proximity with him (even in the same house) over several of the years represented in its pages, having shared the idyll and tumult that was Strasbourg in the late 1970s and 1980s and much more that Lacoue-Labarthe could only allude to in *Phrase*, the task demanded of me a time of maturation. It probably required, as well, the work that I devoted to Maurice Blanchot in the interim, for reasons that will become apparent in the reading that follows. And it required a very significant engagement with the text, one that carried me well beyond the specific theme of infancy. The figurations of infancy and childhood (and of birth) in *Phrase* had to be read from the "history of renunciation" recounted by one who identifies himself in passing, after Hölderlin and Nietzsche, as a "child with grey hair." But I will attempt to show how this history rejoined Blanchot's meditation on what it might mean to write in relation to "the impossible necessary death" which the dying *infans* could figure only in its very effacement. By "renunciation," Lacoue-Labarthe attempted an approach to the acquiescence Blanchot had evoked in his meditation on infancy and to the step or passage it promised. The legacy of infancy, in this case, was one Lacoue-Labarthe had taken over from Blanchot in an effort to bring to language the grounds of his literary experience. It was perhaps in part by Lacoue-Labarthe's intercession (though in ways I cannot pretend to define) that it also became my own.

Infancy. I use the term to designate a condition and a period almost impossible to date because it is time when time is only forming, a phase where language is not yet language (or is coming about as such), where touches (tactile, auditory, visual, even internal) occur that cannot yet be psychically organized for want of a fully defined self, where the fact of desire begins to emerge as a forever preoccupying problem, where imitation and repetition, modulated by play, guide what can barely yet be called learning. It is a state, I would add, into which a young infant with sufficient "maturity" (after who knows how many months) will eventually find itself thrown and from which it will have taken the first mysteriously welcomed and welcoming steps toward a dawning world whose light the philosophers and poets have always struggled to name. For the infant in us, those steps will also always echo in a darkness that is the special concern of the analyst, but also, again, the poet.

There is obviously no dearth of literature, scientific and otherwise, devoted to what is normally conceived within a framework of development (and hence a teleology whose terms find their meaning largely by reference to the ends and the enclosures: a normal maturity). But it is striking how challenging it remains for theorists of all kinds to bring to language the *passage* that is this condition, and what survives of this passage in later life. It is not my purpose in this volume to focus on the question of infancy in itself; indeed, it is ultimately a point of entry into a text that seeks to understand the span between birth and death, when birth itself is understood as exposure to a dying. But it offers a vital access to Lacoue-Labarthe's book, and for this reason I would like to begin by offering a few notes on the *throw* that is infancy from the existential and phenomenological perspectives that informed Lacoue-Labarthe's thinking. This excursus will begin with a discussion of Heidegger that may seem to lead away from the theme of infancy, though I hope to unsettle this impression from the outset by taking my departure from the one genuine "observation" I was able to make regarding the more speculative aspects of the problematic in the years following the composition of *Infant Figures*. The writing of the volume itself had in fact been made possible by other forms of evidence whose status I took up throughout its pages. (In large measure, this was a book of dreams.) I had been convinced that my speculative turn proceeded from a quite insistent experience, an exigency with an origin that was quite "real." But that commitment to the reality of the experience would be confronted with a new test when I faced the terrors of parenting for the first time shortly after the publication of the volume. Would I even be able to recognize something of what I had sought to describe, let alone meet the impossible exigency in the child's cry?

My argument in *Infant Figures* might have even suggested a negative answer to these questions, but an incident with my young son in 2002 offered a possible window onto what I had sought to understand in what I termed infancy. The incident (what I subsequently learned was probably a case of "night fright" or "night terror"[6]) came in early-morning summer hours when Gabriel was just fifteen months old. He had been sleeping on the bed next to me when suddenly he cried out and raced over the edge of the bed. I cannot recall how many times he repeated the fall in the confusion, perhaps it was even just once (the circumstances were so chaotic). But his movements remained desperate and precipitous even after I recovered him from the floor. Once he would allow me to, I held him closely, and then let him rest on his own. I cannot say whether he ever reached a properly waking state. But the ripples of confusion eventually settled, and then three or four minutes after the morning's silence had regathered, I heard him say, quite distinctly, "Uh-oh." He would utter nothing more until daylight.

"Uh-oh" is, of course, a common enough phrase for children of his age (it has even been used as a kind of signature phrase in children's television programming). Gabriel had been using it on almost any occasion when he spilled something, broke something, or even found that something didn't work to his satisfaction. But his use of it this time was distinctive because he did not refer to some situation he had caused or observed and was describing in his infantile way. This time, the accident involved him. I might even say that *he* was the accident, even for himself. He had precipitated from sleep into a kind of fall, a state of falling, and was speaking in some measure after the fact, but still *from that fall*. At least, that is how I heard it. His "uh-oh" echoed with a temporality. He was not reporting on some now past event, and while he had recovered considerably, he was not speaking in the comfort of a regained security or at any reflective distance. His "uh-oh" said, "I've been falling." I could not but hear apprehension in that expression, even a kind of distress. In any case, its manner of bringing the echo of the event into the present so long after its occurrence was profoundly haunting. I would have to say that I have never been quite as gripped by an utterance as by that one.

Did I hear a metaphysical "uh-oh"? Could Gabriel actually have been giving expression to a very early experience of thrownness, or one of its aftershocks: what Heidegger termed *Geworfenheit*?

One might suspect this to be a rather literal interpretation of the Heideggerian notion, but, as it happens, the supposition is not so far-fetched inasmuch as Heidegger speaks metaphorically of the Dasein's "birth" when he evokes what he terms "the facticity" of thrownness. When the Dasein resolves authentically upon its utmost possibilities, carrying up into its project the whole of its existence, from birth to death, as Heidegger says, it carries into its "being toward death" the irreducible fact of its having been cast into existence and into a "falling" that is inseparable from this original throw (the Dasein's *Verfallenheit*). But thrownness itself is given to us in *Being and Time* almost only by this transposition, since thrownness is only known in and with this movement. Heidegger even appears to translate the experience in terms drawn from his description of the Dasein's exposure to its possible impossibility. Thrownness is, for all practical purposes, always already left behind, and this by reason of the futural character of the Dasein's assumption of its being. There are, nevertheless, a few intriguing points of reference, and I will start with brief words on the "facticity of thrownness."[7]

Heidegger defines this phrase for the first time in the context of his discussion of the first form of self-disclosure that is proper to the Dasein's being. He calls this the Dasein's *Befindlichkeit* (Stambaugh gives "attunement" and notes that "disposition" could be an alternative), and tells us that we experience it on an everyday basis in our moods (*Stimmungen*). From an ontological perspective, he says, this is the "primordial" form of disclosure wherein the Dasein is disclosed to itself prior to all cognition and volition, and beyond their range of disclosure (BT, 132/181). In moods, the Dasein is brought before its thrown being as "there." Virtually all moods effect this disclosure by means of a kind of flight from what they disclose, but in every mood there is this disclosure of the being of the there in its "that it is" (*in seinem 'Dass'*).

As Heidegger continues to define what is discovered in the Dasein's *Stimmungen*, he offers us one of the few descriptions of the there. He says that "moods bring Dasein before the fact of its there, which stares directly at it with the inexorability of an enigma" (BT, 132/181). Of this abyss, however, there is no further word. We will have to await another description of thrownness in paragraph 58 for a return to this notion via a discussion of guilt and the call of conscience. There, Heidegger tells us only that when the Dasein assumes its thrownness (something that does not happen once and for all—a crucial point for our consideration of the persistence of something like "infancy"), it also encounters the limits of its power to *be* the ground of its being in the manner to which it is enjoined. Though it is called to assume its being as thrown, Heidegger says, it will *never* have power over itself from the ground up. "This *not* [*Nicht*]," he continues, "belongs to the existential meaning of thrownness" (BT, 273/377). The Dasein's finitude implies that it can never be the author or full "subject" of its existence: "Being a *self*, Dasein, *as* self, is the thrown being. *Not through* itself, but *released to* itself [*an es selbst entlassen*] from the ground in order to be *as the ground*" (BT, 273/377). Thus we may recognize that in the powerlessness encountered in the experience of being-thrown (to the extent that it is disclosed to us), there is an *Entlassen*, a dismissal to, abandoning to, or a releasing to. And the Dasein must in effect "catch itself up" from a being-let-go when it knows itself as thrown into its being-possible. There is probably no saying whether Gabriel's "uh-oh" marked such a recovery.

The powerlessness known by the Dasein in the form of that forbidding "never" is immensely difficult to think in light of the fact that the existential analytic remains largely within the horizon of a thought of production and possibility. Heidegger will insist, nonetheless, on the possibility of the attuned Dasein knowing the abyss that opens in it, and therefore the powerlessness that "determines its being," even as it acts upon its possibilities.[8] Would the understanding of the abyss in the Dasein not therefore entail a relation that would be prior to production or any "act" of understanding even though it would mark it as its limit (and therefore be "prior" in a logical or pre-temporal sense, since it would be related to the opening of temporality itself)? The act of understanding would thus appear to enfold, in some manner, a knowledge of powerlessness that exceeds its own capacity—a knowledge of an exposure that it has *suffered*. Of course, in some measure (or immeasure), this is what Heidegger means by an "attuned understanding." But is this exposure preserved in its abyssal character when it is subsumed within the tragic scenario of being toward a "possible" impossibility (which is the path taken in *Being and Time*—a path that is perhaps more veiling than it is disclosive with respect to the "enigma" Heidegger describes)? Would a genuinely disclosive relation to this uncertain "origin" not have to entail an acquiescence of some kind, a yes? And could it be that such an acquiescence would be part of what originally *enables* understanding—not by empowering, but by allowing or releasing? Would this form of reception release something like a "being-possible" and even any being-toward-death? In brief: does the assumption of finitude, as Heidegger conceived this in the period of the existential analytic, perhaps already imply a form of *Gelassenheit*?

Taking the last cue, I will leap over a vast quantity of material and say just a few brief words regarding a key portion of the "Conversation on a Country Path," a text that is famous for its treatment of the theme of releasement (as *Gelassenheit* is most frequently translated in English). The passage I want to point to follows the assertion that releasement belongs to the essence of thinking, and must therefore be thought *from* that which gives thought to this releasement; thought must therefore approach a movement that is irreducibly prior to it. Of course, such a step can only take the form of a speculative supposition. But Heidegger's interlocutors insist that the language of their conversation leads them in this supposition, and they come thereby to the assertion that truth needs what the human, by essence, lends to it (this is Heidegger's notion of "usage," *der Brauch*). This trait is nothing other than a powerlessness in relation to truth which makes truth's "use" of the human possible:

"Man, for himself, has no capacity over truth, which remains independent of him."[9] There is difference, we might say, because humankind offers to truth an in-capacity that truth needs for its advent. The releasing opening of its "there" in the event of truth remains an im-possible for the Dasein and is assumed in releasement as the very condition of truth.

I note that there is little or no talk of death in this dialogue. A releasement *from* willing and releasement *to* the prior use of the human for the advent of truth does not require, according to this late text, any shattering of the will against impossibility or even any resignation. It does not require a lapsing of any kind. (Lacoue-Labarthe, as we will see, had to think otherwise.) Releasement takes form in a waiting, Heidegger tells us, but it temporalizes out of the past and finds the heart to open to the event from an unfolding experience of engagement that has always already happened. Only from such an "assumption" of an immemorial opening, it seems, could there be something like an authentic opening even to that certain possibility of the Dasein's impossibility. Heidegger declared at the time of the famous *Kehre*, the turn in his thinking, that everything had to be turned about. The notion of usage to which I have alluded articulated this turn, and indicated that even where death is concerned, thought must perhaps learn to take account of what Jean-François Lyotard would come to term its infancy, the original condition of our opening to the event.

Naming Lyotard and alluding to his own approach to the question of infancy brings me back to the question of the nature of the exigency motivating my turn to the question of infancy—a question concerning the actual grounds of this problematic. And given Lyotard's more psychoanalytically inflected approach to this topic (more psychoanalytical, in any case, than the one offered in *Phrase*), I am prompted to recall that Gabriel's "uh-oh" experience came at approximately one and a half years—the same age Freud offered for the occasion of the "primal scene" in one of his most daring speculative constructions of this event. For Lyotard, the "throw" Heidegger evokes in seeking to account for an initiating movement was always inseparable from the experience of desire, whose *real* character stemmed from the psyche's relation to what he would refer to by a psychoanalytic shorthand as "the thing." The reality in question, however, was inseparable from the experience of ontological difference. On this basis, he could take up Hannah Arendt's reflections on natality and speak with some ease of infancy as entailing some "debt." He was here developing a thought of infancy in relation to the notion of finitude that I have sought to evoke in these pages.[10]

To elaborate the connection between the question of desire and its link to ontological difference, I am tempted to delve deeply into Freud's intriguing case study on the one he named the Wolf Man. I will refrain from a full textual engagement, however, and simply underscore a point made allusively by Lacan with respect to this study.[11] I refer here to Freud's extraordinary insistence on the *real* grounds of his construction of the primal scene from the analytic work that proceeded from the analysis of the dream of the wolves (a dream whose own starkly "real" character pointed to some real event in the past).[12] Freud was actually willing to compromise on what would have been the empirical "facts" in the latter part of his case study (surprisingly enough [TCH, 256]), but he would not compromise on his claim that what was behind the affect expressed in the dream was the sudden formation or crystallization of a knowledge concerning something very real: "the existence of castration."[13] Let me recall simply Freud's conclusion that the child's eager wish for presents on a Christmas eve (also the eve of his fourth birthday) had given way to the implications of another wish involving his father that the child drew from his belated elaboration of an earlier scene of sexual activity he had observed involving his parents. Developing the implications of this wish in remarkably precise terms, Freud could not help but note that the positions presumably assumed by the parents could recall that of sheep, which the young child had seen in considerable number on his parents' summer estate—an association that led to an evocation of death (for the father's herd had suffered an epidemic which was only accelerated by a program of inoculation). Associations with illness, his own and his mother's, indicated that an exposure to the fact of mortality was not separable from what the child had supposedly witnessed in that earliest "scene" to which he was exposed at eighteen months, and helped determine the meaning of what Freud insistently referred to as castration.

But a no less striking allusion to an experience of "reality" emerges quite late in Freud's analysis, when he comes to account for the patient's cycle of brief recovery after the administration of an enema (necessitated by the fact that the patient, in a certain period, could not pass a bowel movement without such an intervention from a male nurse). The world, the patient would complain, was normally "veiled" except for a brief period after the enema. At which point, he saw the world clearly and experienced a kind of rebirth.

> If we look into the matter more closely we cannot help remarking that in this condition which he laid down for this recovery, the patient was simply repeating the state of affairs at the time of the so-called primal scene [. . . .] The tearing of the veil was analogous to the opening of his eyes [in the scene] and to the opening of the window [in the dream]. The primal scene had become transformed into the necessary condition for his recovery. (TCH, 258)

This administered, repeated birth to the day (partaking of an early rhythm that had taken in infancy, captured in the dream with the opening of the windows and subsequently with the beating of butterfly wings) was nothing other, I would suggest, than a rehearsing of the original opening to reality.

"Infancy," as I noted above, is the time of such first openings to the day—a time for which the "primal scene" offers perhaps our closest approach to something like a date, though no verification of the coincidence of an affect linked to desire and a primal experience of ontological difference can be anticipated: for no evidence will confirm the possibility of "evidence" itself. Lyotard, as I have noted, would affirm the link, and would come to claim that a surviving capacity for such an opening to the world would be the condition of an opening to what he called the event. The first "throw" (of desire?), he concluded, had an ontological import whose cast would echo throughout a life, both in various forms of difficulty and in a propensity for astonishment informing the faculty of judgment.

Lacoue-Labarthe, as we will see, describes the throw of infancy in quite comparable terms, and like Lyotard (or like Blanchot), he will seek to draw from the "openings" experienced in infancy the capacity of affirming the gift known there—this, despite the advancing onset of terrible incapacities also linked to the fate or destiny (singular, but also of its time, in a sense defined most powerfully, for Lacoue-Labarthe, by Friedrich Hölderlin) into which he had been thrown. "Phrase" names the articulation of these possibilities and impossibilities, their *writing*, and *Phrase* seeks to engage the "freeing" part of this writing (enabling what Hölderlin named a "free use of the proper") in such a way as to find the possibility of an honorable and even joyful assumption of the tragic course of mortal existence.

These terms can only take on reality or concreteness in the course of the reading to follow.[14] But the peculiar status of this concreteness should be acknowledged from the outset, for, as I will reiterate in the course of the analysis, there can be no final establishment of the meaning of the terms in question through hermeneutic or theoretical (let alone empirical) demonstration.

Their "adequacy" to lived experience must remain on the order of supposition and their value can perhaps only finally be gauged from what I would term their *resonance* (an evocative force whose pitch is defined by unsparing critical acuity—by which I mean to say that no compromise is made here with respect to the rights of the concept, even if the latter cannot suffice for what is brought to language). Too much of *Phrase*, in fact, is devoted to the unsayable for there to be any proper grounding of its language in a traditional sense. This unsayable is what Lacoue-Labarthe will not (despite astonishing candor in many respects) and cannot bring to full discovery or intelligibility. And there are compelling reasons—probed by Lacoue-Labarthe himself—for accepting his conclusion that this unsayable or unavowable cannot be brought to some adequate account. *Phrase* explores this impossibility of an adequate understanding or translation in multiple ways, offering itself in significant measure as a text *about* the possibility of rendering the experiences that lie at its heart, even as it seeks to approach them. The text thus takes more than one path to the silences that haunt it, and none of these paths ever meet in quite the same place. The end/the origin sought *refuse* themselves, and the discursive paths taken are irreducible to one another.

One of the paths is literary, though the term "literary" itself must remain broad since it involves here an important share of poetry (a genre Lacoue-Labarthe holds in the highest regard, as well as the highest suspicion), but also writing of a more properly dramatic character. This path is privileged because the silences themselves belong to what he names literature. Of the "phrase" he seeks in this book, he declares that it will have never been pronounced by him, that it will have remained haunting: "That aborted pronunciation, that haunting, I call, decidedly, literature" (P, 12). There is an element of fiat in that decision, but its force is subject to almost immediate qualification as Lacoue-Labarthe remarks, only two pages later, that "literature" must also name an infinite paraphrase, an "approximation" of the forever unpronounceable. The literature of *Phrase* moves in the space of that answering form of approach, that *nearing saying.* As a literary effort, it remarks constantly upon the limits of that effort and its own separation from itself as "literature."

But *Phrase* is also a book of theoretical reflection whose background (in decades of painstaking philosophical, psychoanalytic, artistic, musicological, and political thought pursued in seminars in Strasbourg and published in influential critical volumes) resonates profoundly throughout.[15] A very great deal of this reflection, however, is latent in this book, and here again Lacoue-Labarthe appears to want to mark the limits of theoretical inquiry before the experiences he seeks to approach and bring into a "just" language. Lacoue-Labarthe is in fact interested in what escapes the hold of the theory he masters so well, which is nothing other than an experience of his own finitude.

Approaching this multiple, even fragmented piece of writing, I have sought to honor the privilege given to the literary, and the immense effort dedicated to it. This is one reason for devoting the principal part of this analysis to the "story" ("*l'histoire— . . . it is perhaps, unfortunately, a kind of myth*" [P, 13]) that traverses most of the volume. I seek to limn the significance of this story for the larger design of *Phrase*, taking as my point of entry and special focus the topic of infancy. My ambition is modest, in this respect, since I seek primarily to draw forth the resonance of its "approximating" terms and to suggest what has *happened* in it, thereby providing a legible outline for *Phrase* as a whole. But it is in that resonance that I seek the justness of this text and the concreteness of its language as an act of approximation in relation to the "realities" at its heart. On the margins, I place ongoing commentary on the theoretical and philosophical elements of this highly reflective piece of writing that is preoccupied with the relation between literature and "literature" noted above, and that was always inseparable from a work of thought. At a later point in this exposition, I allow this reflective mode into the body of the text, thus punctuating it and preparing an ending (or the reading of a possible ending).

It would actually be possible to read *Phrase* as having been "theorized" before its writing (I will indicate moments where this possibility shows itself), but this gesture would require a searching consideration of the existential bases of Lacoue-Labarthe's drive to theorize in writing of notorious complexity in the first place. In any case, theory does not deserve a subservient status in a reading of the work, which is why I have allowed endnotes such a prominent place in my commentary. At the same time, I have sought to give the story, in all its complexity, an intelligible exposition, and it is for this reason that I have not interrupted the exposition with long theoretical statements.

I would add that Lacoue-Labarthe's own reserve regarding the unpronounceable (the unsayable, the unavowable—each of these should be heard in their full resonance with respect to aspects of this text) has prompted in me a style of writing that is perhaps of a particularly demanding character. I experience this writing as taut and condensing, like the effort to draw a bow. I have written a text that I hope will not overly violate what Lacoue-Labarthe preserves from interpretative grasp and even withholds in acts of discretion, seeking instead, by a kind of precise articulation, the resonance to which I have referred. By drawing a literary reading into proximity with theoretical reflection, I seek to bring to sound what lies between philosophy and literature in the life of a writer who devoted much of his life to both philosophy and literature. I could only aim to do this as exactly and sensitively as possible. An interpretative effort could have taken many other forms, surely; but I am not sure I myself could have done it otherwise. In my many years of work with Lacoue-Labarthe, I learned a phrasing that proved *necessary* in this context.

I would like to thank Alejandro Cerda Rueda for his generous support for the original idea of this project; I am immensely grateful that he is bringing a version of it into Spanish. I would also like to express my warm gratitude to Michael Eng for a characteristically attentive critical reading and my appreciation to Avital Ronell for her efforts on behalf of the legacy left by Lacoue-Labarthe. Finally, I want to acknowledge the always deepening debt to Edith Doron, who has helped keep me alert to those "curious developments" that present themselves in infancy.

NOTES

1. Philippe Lacoue-Labarthe, *Phrase* (Paris: Christian Bourgois Éditeur, 2000).

2. *Infant Figures: The Death of the* Infans *and Other Scenes of Origin* (Stanford: Stanford University Press, 2000).

3. I cite the passage from which these words come (a fictive exchange in which Blanchot explicitly questions the term "scene") as well as "(A Primal Scene?)" itself in the opening pages of my analysis.

4. I will note some of these in the course of my analysis of *Phrase*. The first appearance of what became the final publication is a text itself entitled *Phrase*, published by Orange Export Ltd., Collection "Chutes," 1977.

5. Jean-Christophe Bailly, *La véridiction: sur Philippe Lacoue-Labarthe* (Paris: Christian Bourgois Éditeur, 2011), 15. *Phrase* was published in the same series, Détroits, which Lacoue-Labarthe and Bailly edited with their friend Michel Deutsch.

6. The condition is apparently a rather common one, if somewhat mysterious in its provenance. Freud makes reference to it in a letter to Fliess of August 1890: "My daughter has night frights that

make her wake up in the night screaming. What makes her so afraid? She has no idea, the poor little one, and we don't either, of course" (cited by Mikkel Borch-Jacobsen in "In statut nascendi," *Hypnoses*, ed. Mikkel Borch-Jacobsen, Eric Michaud, and Jean-Luc Nancy [Paris: Éditions Galilée, 1984], 73).

7. I cite here the relevant passage from Joan Stambaugh's translation of *Being and Time* (Albany: State University of New York Press, 2010), 132.

> We shall call this character of being of Dasein which is veiled in its whence and whither, but in itself all the more openly disclosed, this 'that it is,' the *thrownness* [*Geworfenheit*] of this being into its there; it is thrown in such a way that it is the there as being-in-the-world. The expression thrownness is meant to suggest the *facticity of its being delivered over.* [. . .] *Facticity is not the factuality of the* factum brutum *of something objectively present, but is a characteristic of the being of Dasein taken on in existence, although initially thrust aside.*

Heidegger's insistence that the "that" is not something factual that might be observed like other intraworldly facts is critical for the issue I evoked at the outset in speaking of the reality of infancy. Note that subsequent citations of this translation in the body of the text will be indicated by the abbreviation BT. I will provide the page number of the translation first, followed by a reference to the corresponding page of Vol. 2 of the *Gesamtausgabe*, ed. Friedrich-Wilhelm von Hermann (Frankfurt am Main: Vittorio Klostermann, 1976); the present citation is from p. 180.

8. I cite here from the conclusion of "The Essence of Ground," where Heidegger describes what he terms the "primordial" movement of freedom by which the Dasein is given to itself and is given to understand that its abyssal character, the "nothing" of its foundation, can never be eliminated. He notes here that this notion of freedom allows us to recognize that the earthly Dasein subject to attunement in moods must be understood as freely so attuned, and then concludes: "The fact

that [Dasein] has the possibility of being a self, and has this factically in keeping with its freedom in each case; the fact *that* transcendence temporalizes itself as a primordial occurrence, does not stand in the power of this freedom itself. Yet such impotence (thrownness) is not first the result of beings forcing themselves upon Dasein, but rather determines Dasein's being as such" (trans. William McNeill in *Pathmarks* [Cambridge: Cambridge University Press, 1998], 135).

9. From *Discourse on Thinking*, Section II, "Conversation on a Country Path About Thinking," trans. John M. Anderson and E. Hans Freund (New York: Harper and Row, 1966), 84.

10. My remarks on Lyotard's work on the question of infancy are based on an essay first published in *Yale French Studies* in 2001 (YFS99, 44–61): "Jean-François's Infancy." I have expanded this essay considerably for the Spanish translation (forthcoming from Paradiso Editores, Mexico City), which will include the translation of this reading of *Phrase*.

11. I refer to Lacan's remarks in chapter 5 ("Tuché and Automaton") of *The Four Fundamental Concepts of Psycho-Analysis*, ed. Jacques-Alain Miller, trans. Alan Sheridan (New York: W. W. Norton, 1981), 53–64. There, he evokes the case of the Wolf Man at the outset of a discussion that is preceded by the declaration that "No praxis is more oriented towards that which, at the heart of experience, is the kernel of the real than psycho-analysis" (53).

12. Freud: "We know from our experience interpreting dreams that this sense of reality [*Wirklichkeitsgefühl*] carries a particular significance with it. It assures us that some part of the latent material of the dream is claiming in the dreamer's memory to possess the quality of reality [*Wirklichkeit*], that is, that the dream relates to an occurrence [*Begebenheit*] that really [*wirklich*] took place and was not merely imagined." (I cite from Sigmund Freud, *Three Case Histories* [New York: Macmillan Publishing, 1963], 190–191; subsequent citations in the text will be indicated with the abbreviation TCH). Later in the analysis, Freud appeals for the reader's *provisional* belief in the reality (*Realität*) of the scene (TCH, 196), and reverts to the same term, *Realität*, for a general discussion of the patient's sense of conviction regarding the reality of the scenes underlying dreams (TCH, 209). He

will also affirm their "lived reality" (*erlebten Realität*). Finally, Freud will link his discussion of primal scenes in this case to the general considerations of *Introductory Lectures on Psychoanalysis* and refer, in this respect, to the *Realwert* of primal scenes (TCH, 214).

13. "The material of the analysis shows that there is one condition that this picture must satisfy. It must have been calculated to create the conviction of the existence of castration" (TCH, 194). In the long footnote that summarizes Freud's interpretation of the Wolf Man's dream, he will word this conviction as follows: "So there really is such a thing as castration" (*Es gibt also wirklich eine Kastration*) (TCH, 201).

14. Here again, we meet Freud's concerns in his case of the Wolf Man, for he tells us explicitly and repeatedly that his problem is one of finding a form of presentation that could produce in the reader a conviction comparable to that of the patient himself with respect to the reality of the elements of his experience brought forth by Freud.

15. In 1990, I had the pleasure of presenting an important segment of this work in an edited volume, *Typography: Philosophy, Mimesis, Politics* (Cambridge: Harvard University Press).

THE LIFE OF A PHRASE

Infancy, Renunciation, Passing

In 1976, Philippe Lacoue-Labarthe and Mathieu Benezet invited Maurice Blanchot to contribute to *Première Livraison*, at that time a journal with limited circulation. They received, in response, the initial version of the brief narrative that Blanchot would republish a few years thereafter in *The Writing of the Disaster*.[1] The latter publication introduced only a few alterations, but drew the original title into a parenthesis and suspended it with a question mark, leaving the following:

> (A primal scene?) *You who live later, close to a heart that beats no more, suppose, suppose this: the child—is he seven years old, or eight perhaps?—standing, drawing the curtain and, through the window pane, looking. What he sees: the garden, the wintry trees, the wall of a house: while he sees, no doubt in a child's way, his play space, he tires and slowly looks up toward the ordinary sky, with its clouds, the grey light, the day pallid and without depth.*
>
> *What happens then: the sky, the same sky, suddenly open, absolutely black and absolutely empty, revealing (as though the pane had broken) such an absence that all has since always and forevermore been lost in it, to the point that there is affirmed and there dissipates there the vertiginous knowledge that nothing is what there is, and first of all nothing beyond. The unexpected in this scene*

> *(its interminable feature) is the feeling of happiness that immediately submerges the child, the ravaging joy to which he can bear witness only by tears, an endless streaming of tears. He is thought to suffer a childish distress; attempts are made to console him. He says nothing. He will live henceforth in the secret. He will weep no more.*

The appearance of this version roughly halfway through *The Writing of the Disaster* was prepared by nine pages of theoretical and philosophical reflections that implicitly (though across the borders of an insistently fragmentary exposition) linked Blanchot's fictional casting of the after-experience of an "immemorial death" to the meditations of D. W. Winnicott and Serge Leclaire on what Blanchot invites us to think as "the death of the *infans*." They also addressed a difficulty faced by the (Hegelian) dialectic in seeking to subsume in negation a passing that renders it both possible and impossible: what Blanchot named "the impossible necessary death."[2] This impossibility, he suggested, only reinforced the exigency of a singular figuration that would necessarily *insist* in psychic life, even in its effacement in the traces of what Blanchot named a writing.

> A child already dead dies, of a murderous death; an infant of which we know nothing, even if we qualify him as marvelous, terrifying, tyrannical or indestructible. Except this: that the possibility of speech and life would depend, through death and murder, on the relation of singularity established fictively with a mute past, to the hither side of history, thus outside the past, for which the eternal infans becomes a figure, at the same time as it steals away from it. "A child is being killed." Let us not be mistaken about this present: it signifies that the operation could never take place once and for all, that it is not accomplished

> at any privileged moment of time, that it operates inoperably and thus tends to be none but the very time that destroys (effaces) time, an effacement, or a destruction, or a gift that has always already avowed itself in the precession of a Saying outside any said, a word of writing whereby this effacement, far from effacing itself in its turn, is perpetuated without term even in the *interruption* that constitutes its mark.[3]

I cite these stunning lines in order to establish the bridge between the reading of *Phrase* to come and the reflection on infancy that I pursued in *Infant Figures*. I also want to prepare the reader's ear for the repeated recourse to the motif of infancy and related themes in Lacoue-Labarthe's text, beginning with the striking image from which it starts, dated July 1976 (following Lacoue-Labarthe's usage in this volume, which is to date each part, each "Phrase"):

> and because it is manifest that it is, in you, elsewhere,
> no place of concern to you, that this streams
> or collapses (I don't know, I think of a visage
>   exhausted, betrayed, covered in tears,
> etc.—in fact, of supplication). (P, 9)

Of course, the link to Blanchot does not exhaust what appears in these words. Indeed, they may have been written without immediate reference to Blanchot's text. But we might well imagine a stronger connection if we pursue the hypothesis that Blanchot's text somehow released the writing that would become *Phrase*—in which case, Blanchot's brief narrative would have been the original scene for *Phrase* itself, a kind of focal point for a broader textual involvement that was not without an agonistic dimension. Implicit citations of Blanchot abound in *Phrase*, but one section, describing a scene of intense struggle, is dedicated to Blanchot and quotes insistently from another section of *The Writing of the Disaster* devoted, in reflective dialogue, to the "primal scene" offered earlier in Blanchot's volume.[4] It is one among several segments that reveal just how deeply Lacoue-Labarthe was engaged with Blanchot's text (a fact not otherwise strongly visible until the posthumous publication of *Agonie terminée, agonie interminable, sur Maurice Blanchot*[5]). We will have to return to the question of the nature of this engagement. For now, let me merely offer a last recollection of the lines from which Lacoue-Labarthe drew for the section of *Phrase* to which I have just referred, "*(L'émoi)*." They name, via their evocation of the drying of the "endless flow of tears" that bore witness to the child's overwhelming joy, the dis-interest Lacoue-Labarthe sought in what he termed "renunciation." And they name what we may feel to have been at stake for Lacoue-Labarthe in his effort to write this extraordinary book: survival.

> The ever-suspended question: having died of this "ability to die" which gives him joy and devastation, did he survive—or rather, what does to survive mean then, if not to be sustained by an assent to refusal, by the exhaustion of feeling, and to live withdrawn from any interest in oneself, disinterested, thinned out to a state of utter calmness, expecting nothing?—Consequently, waiting and watching, for suddenly wakened and, knowing this full well henceforth, never wakeful enough.[6]

~

How, then, shall we approach Lacoue-Labarthe's testimonial effort in *Phrase* and what it gives to us of an infancy? The path indicated is that of the story (*histoire*) of a renunciation (P, 13), offered in the course of the twenty-one sections of this text: a story, or a history—even though the fragmented, varying character of its writing and the extra-temporal character of its events (the times of "birth" and "death" do not conform to chronology) make any reliance upon a narrative order fundamentally problematic. The motif of infancy is powerfully recurrent in *Phrase*, as I have noted, but what Lacoue-Labarthe evokes with this term cannot be taken simply as some stage or moment within a standard temporal schema or developmental order, however insistently it presents itself as initial in the psychic life presented. Moreover, like "phrase" or "caesura," "infancy" finally resists discursive hold or theoretical construction. No conceptual definition can quite secure a consistent meaning for these terms which Lacoue-Labarthe sought to apply to a profoundly overwhelming experience. In fact, Lacoue-Labarthe himself did not believe such a meaning could be found, as a significant theoretical statement appended to Phrase II makes quite clear; the question presented by what he names "phrase" cannot ever be properly formulated (P, 20). We are thus left with the task of following the way these motifs are deployed and brought to speech in *Phrase*, and for a minimum of intelligibility we are pretty much obliged to follow the broken story Lacoue-Labarthe offers, his construction of the *exposure* he repeatedly suffered in and as what he came to name *literature*, and his highly reflected account of the way in which a decisive chapter of this literary experience opened and closed in relation with another whose name is given to us as "Claire." From something more or less than a story, therefore—and for this all the more poignant, all the more painful—I will seek to trace Lacoue-Labarthe's incipient thought of infancy and what the experience in which it echoed required of him in the manner of what he came to call *renunciation*. I will thus follow Lacoue-Labarthe's effort to write the allegory that is *Phrase* itself.

From the outset, however, we encounter a difficulty that goes to the heart of the "story of renunciation" and is an essential factor in both the undoing it recounts and the "unworking" that afflicts it as a story. It manifests itself narratively, but derives essentially from the import of that latent pre-inscription ("phrase") that he claims is determining for his existence. Addressing this difficulty, if only through a work of provisional definition and by a rapid sketch of the narrative, seems a prerequisite for achieving coherence and legibility in the necessarily brief (too brief, however long) account to come. The challenges involved here will make this necessary introduction rather dense, but my hope is that this initial step will ease the way for a reading that seeks to follow closely the movement and language of a very beautiful text.

We begin with "phrase," then, a term whose position as both title and repeated section-heading (each of the twenty-one sections of the volume thus presumably partakes in some manner of what is named with the term—each one *phrases* in the invention or sounding of the sought phrase) mark it as *defining* both for the material presented and its mode of presentation. To what does the term refer in this volume—bearing in mind Lacoue-Labarthe's own admission that its provenance and character ultimately escaped him? Let us describe it, again provisionally and somewhat abstractly (seeking to evoke *what* so defines—though it is no "thing"—and leaving aside as yet its presentation, the way it comes to be written in the text), as what destines or "sentences" in an individual existence: something less than an articulated saying and present to experience as barely more than a latent, pre-scribing idiograph. But let us also recognize that this already overly formal definition cannot be secured by reference to linguistics, music, philosophy, or psychology (even with a psychoanalytic turn that would open onto the preconscious or the unconscious). The term calls upon us, rather, to draw from all of these fields from the *ground* of their possible pertinence for the constitution of a subjectivity—this "ground" (or non-ground) requiring for its conception something comparable to what Jacques Derrida entertained and deconstructed in his earlier work under the name of a "grammatology."[7] Lacoue-Labarthe had himself traced this formidable methodological imperative in an essay on Theodor Reik composed very shortly before he undertook the writing that became *Phrase*, noting very precisely at its opening where the questions undertaken inevitably escaped his theoretical hold.[8] *Phrase*, as I have suggested, will repeat this indication of a limit, implicitly inviting us to carry the questioning further. And we can, perhaps, carry a form of speculation about this "originary" experience a bit further along some of the lines Lacoue-Labarthe has drawn. But Lacoue-Labarthe makes it clear that the limit he reached was ultimately not traversable *in theory* inasmuch as it was finally defined by nothing other than the finitude of the human Dasein, as Heidegger offered it to thought (refusing it, in the same gesture, to the grasp of any conceptual articulation as he traced the limits of the metaphysics of subjectivity and representation). The term "finitude" doesn't settle anything, of course, but it will serve to indicate the level at which Lacoue-Labarthe sought to move/to write in this auto-bio-graphical attempt, and it offers perhaps the most fitting rhetorical register for this initial work of definition (all the more so as Lacoue-Labarthe's primary philosophical reference in the initial period of the composition of this book was in fact Heidegger[9]). It thus leads me to recast what has been offered thus far with a definition of "phrase" that remains still too philosophical, but is perhaps suggestive of what Lacoue-Labarthe sought to bring to writing, which is nothing other than the experience of his own finitude and what he knew of a fateful destiny.

"Phrase," as Lacoue-Labarthe sought to present it, then, would name the schematizing element of that *liminal exposure* in which a subject finds a relation to itself and to the world in both affect and understanding. It is the always singular articulation ("writing") of a pre-symbolic inheritance which inscribes itself with the subject's advent or birth to existence, thereby bringing something like a distinctive rhythm and pitch to the experience that takes form there, as well as a more fateful tenor (which will figure in *Phrase* almost as a familial curse, finally articulated for Lacoue-Labarthe by his mother at the time of her death[10]). Never given, never fully accessible, always *haunting* even in its return, it would be determinant in configuring what we might call the *line* of a singular existence. It would be something like the characterizing signature of what Heidegger referred to with his use of the word "Dasein." Only literature, in Lacoue-Labarthe's understanding, could begin to catch the incisive rhythm, pitch and tenor of this latent phrasing that shapes the individual subject (or truly *think* it, hence the final futility of this work of definition); indeed, he named the exposing insistence of phrase itself "literature" (P, 11–17).[11]

But if "phrase" has a conditioning or determining force, it is no less, in Lacoue-Labarthe's experience, de-constitutive. It is the writing of that exposure that Heidegger named in his earlier work "transcendence," as I have tried to suggest, but it is also *exposing*. Its periodic return or insistence thus brings Lacoue-Labarthe back to a state comparable to that immemorial condition to which Blanchot assigned the figure of the dying *infans*. The descriptions of that seizure (or the accompanying *émoi*—as in the case of the section devoted to Blanchot) that is the coming of phrase for Lacoue-Labarthe strongly recall that condition. And though the overwhelming character of this state is not necessarily linked to infancy itself (some of the experiences of affliction and intense dispossession described have nothing "infantile" about them), Lacoue-Labarthe repeatedly makes this connection, implicitly suggesting that "phrase" must have found its first articulation from the earliest phases of the subject's pre-history, and *taken* in the "first" advent to the day. Bearing a trace of this "origin," phrase always calls back from that site, even as it dictates an irrevocable decline.[12] Lacoue-Labarthe's most poignant and most moving evocation of infancy in fact returns to what we must probably take as an early articulation or "phrasing" of phrase. It comes, as we will see, via relation to the other—via what this relation gives of a return to the origin. But Lacoue-Labarthe's descriptions of the advent of phrase outside this relation stress a terrible, debilitating exposure to disaggregating forces that overwhelm him as subject of this experience. Thus, to put this generally, if phrase might be said to *distinguish*, or characterize a singular existence ("separating it out," in some respects), it also separates the subject from itself and exposes it to a form of disappropriation. For Lacoue-Labarthe, this occurred in a manner that was progressively degenerating and isolating. Here again, Blanchot's lead, as Lacoue-Labarthe understood it, was decisive, though this literary and theoretical precedent lessened in no way the extremity of the suffering Lacoue-Labarthe brought to the text.

Of course, the singular, exposing force of what Lacoue-Labarthe sought to describe as "phrase" helped determine the very possibility and the extraordinary strength of the passion for that other whose name, as I have noted, the text repeatedly spells for us. It gave Lacoue-Labarthe over to a relation with a destiny of its own. It was also the condition of impossibility for this same relation, ultimately forcing a form of abandonment (and this too will be a form of renunciation) that turns a shared exposure (relatively brief, all told)—and even a shared phrase—into disunion. The relation, however imposing and inevitable in its inception, will ultimately prove to have been something *exceptional* in an inexorable course of experience. One can hardly help but want to read it otherwise, particularly if one writes from some degree of familiarity with the individuals portrayed, and there is also no denying the lasting beauty of what occurred there, the memory of its event. But there is no way to save, to "lift" this terrible account of a foundering in a finally solitary, albeit exposed, existence, no way of retaining a final, redemptive dimension of the separation the one takes in relation to the other, even via the motif of renunciation, whose promise orients the narrative, or via a reference to a theory of the tragic. For renunciation cannot be understood as ever *achieved* in this story, though it furtively appears there. Even the term "survival," in this perspective, presents a challenge, though I will try to indicate its signs in the concluding pages of this essay.

We might now state the core of the difficulty afflicting the story of renunciation formulaically by saying that the narrating subject's destiny, as defined by this phrase that he seeks to bring into expression or articulation (into a *prose*), cannot finally, in a lasting manner, compose with that fateful relation he knows with the loved other, even though it may only have been by this relation that the singular phrase defining his existence could ever have been brought to writing. "Phrase," *a* phrase, in fact sounds in each of what we might call the subject's two lines of experience as delineated in *Phrase*: that of his insistently solitary course, and that of the relationship (for the relationship, too, as we will see, is "phrased," presumably by the conjugation of the two destinies in play[13]). But it is difficult to say that the one enters into a true accord with the other for more than a brief interval whose span resists any dating. Granted, this is a highly theoretical way of expressing the tragic condition of a great many relationships: the conditions of their possibility are also those of their impossibility. But here, once again, we have the complication that it is only by the relationship that access (by renunciation) to the singular lines of a destiny is given. And to put this more precisely, it appears that it is only by the writing (the "phrasing") of the tragic destiny of this relationship that the imperative of renunciation can take form and be assumed as the path to the sounding of "phrase" for the singular subject. So, to repeat, what Lacoue-

Labarthe names "phrase" renders both possible and impossible the relation by which its renounced saying is approached (in writing). And hence the terrible challenge of *Phrase*: it can only *align* two experiences of phrase, offering them more than once as indistinguishable, but failing to hold or sustain this relation (as a subtle song, let us say, or a composed articulation, even a "myth") for anything beyond a brief period, even suggesting that it cannot be so held. This is why the line of this narrative as a whole is fundamentally broken, fundamentally fragmentary—why the disaggregating line of the narrating subject's separation from himself is the dominant motif of this frequently poignant but often brutal autobiographical effort.

FROM THE BEGINNING

The difficulty I have sought to outline is legible in the very first section of *Phrase*, which we can perhaps now begin to approach, despite its extreme density.

> . . . let—let come (give way, probably,
> or well up, though barely)
> what will not come and cannot arrive, for want
> if only of what would be a sure bank
> and because it is manifest that it is elsewhere, in you,
> no place of concern to you, that this streams
> or collapses (I think of a visage that is exhausted,
> betrayed, covered in tears,
> etc.—of supplication, in fact),
> let, yes, let age and decline in you
> what did not take place:
> we are held to it, constrained to it, as to
> the irrevocable, which, the one forever following
> the other, separates us, the one apart from the other
> binds us;

> for our exposure is that the echo, in us, should be
> of practically no voice, the things, around us
> (this garden, for example, there,
> this field, always the same)
> the trace, of course, of no passing. (P, 9–10)

In the simplest terms: what is the link between the relation to the "infant figure" that appears *on the verge* of a self-relation and as a *near saying* of supplication (the figure, if it is one, is infant in its emergence, but what has emerged, without ever fully coming into being, is also declining, while the flow of its expression is failing) and "our" binding to what is termed simply "the irrevocable"? Does this "as to" suggest some form of identity between "what does not take place" and the irrevocable, or some form of similitude in the respective relations of constraint? The failing emergence is ascribed to an individual ("you"—but the speaker and the addressee are undefined), while the binding that separates shows itself for at least two in the echo, or trace, of almost nothing. The first address (to you) may well have "general" import for those in the relation (and is perhaps made possible by the relation, the emergent itself being in some way *of* that relation), or for anyone at all. But with respect to the linking term ("constraint"), we know only that relation to what has not taken place holds "us" (and again there is an ambiguity—is this in general, for humanity in general, or for those in the relation of binding/separation?) *just as* (*de même qu'à*) we are held to the irrevocable. There is no common term here beyond what we might import from the broader context of the book by suggesting that in both cases we have to do with an experience of dying. A Blanchotian formulation might allow us to suggest in addition that one (the one who speaks) can speak to a solitary passing in the other by virtue of the shared *dying-with* named in the last lines. But the relation between the two experiences remains without further articulation (without relation, we might say) and hardly more than one of apposition. The two lines of experience, as they are presented here, simply *near* one another. They will appear to be indistinguishable at points, and they will virtually converge as the text approaches what I have termed the end of the narrated relation, but their lasting union is fatally prohibited.

I should emphasize that we have, in these lines, an extraordinarily poised, if somber, formulation of the relational character of "dying-with" (and what this perhaps brings to a relation of love).[14] Something essential may well be indicated here about the abyssal foundations of human relation in general. But in *this* relation, this "slow catastrophe / or this exodus" (from the last lines of Phrase I [P, 10]), the implications are forbidding. As it happens, the lines we have just read are spoken from a point of greatest intimacy; they do not reflect the extremity of the disaster to come.

Phrase II and its "Post-Scriptum," which contains the theoretical statement to which I have alluded, will present more directly but no less aporetically the singular complication I have attempted to indicate as it proceeds to define phrase from the ground of the narrating subject's singular experience of literature before linking this description (aligning?—conjoining?) with that of the passion known in encounter with the other. I will move relatively slowly over Lacoue-Labarthe's steps here in view of the arresting character of what he seeks to introduce with the term "phrase."

Here are the first lines of Phrase II, "(Clarification)":

> Phrase: what has pronounced itself in me—afar, else-
> where, almost
> outside—for a very long time,
> ever since the possibility of forgetting was given to
> me, I believe,
> I call it literature. (P, 11)

The term "forgetting" here has an unmistakable Bataillan/Blanchotian resonance (though Hölderlin is also audible, as we will see). Forgetting would belong to the very opening of a literary thought, and phrase would be the saying onto which it opens. This saying, Lacoue-Labarthe continues, is without meaning, usually without content, barely articulated, and almost always the *same*, or so it seems in its various "modulations" according to the states of being of the one for whom it sounds (various *Stimmungen*, we might say, but from this latter notion we must not exclude physical states such as fatigue that cannot be understood merely in vital terms, since "dying" in this context cannot be understood essentially or entirely in relation to the forces available for the interests of "life"). Never having quite captured it, Lacoue-Labarthe—and let us also use his name for the writing subject of this literary experience—proposes, in an apparent evocation of Mallarmé, that it is something on the order of a *legend*, a murmur from an ancient history that has sounded through generations. But the burden of this awaiting legacy will have never found articulation in the tongue to which this writing subject ceaselessly comes to be as a self in relation to the things and beings of the world. Mallarmé has thus been called up with Heidegger to give us both the destinal and the fateful character of phrase as the condition of possibility of a *poietic* existence (even, as we will see, a "dwelling") whose grounds of receptivity is named in the subsequent passage:

> Thus I believe, rather, that it still seeks to take form,
> the phrase,
> and that it has never, in sum, quite made it. Never,
> in any case, have I heard it. On the contrary, I
> suspect that if sometimes I happen to hear—words,
> a diction, music—it is because
> of this phrase which awaits, indefinitely,
> its fall and its closing. (P, 12)

What will have been created with and from this hearing (of words, diction, music), in the lines *sustained* and *drawn out* in this hearing, both in existence and its writing, is what, of phrase, (he) will have been:

> *At the limit, that is to say at those moments of terrifying forgetting when the slightest winter's light on a wall, the poor grass of a garden, the water of a stream is, in hiatus, the pure sign that I am going to die, I could say, and this too would be pronounced, in silence, would let itself be taken into the phrase: I will have been a phrase.*
>
> *Or rather, there will have been phrase, this phrase—which will have haunted me, which I will never have pronounced.* (P, 12)

The dying insistence of this phrase ("which awaits, indefinitely, its fall and its closing"), a waiting that will later be evoked with a near concluding note from Beethoven's String Quartet no. 15, is thus carried beautifully, after an extended pause, into this more immediate presentation of the imminence of death.[15] But of what death is the sign given? There is surely a glimpse of mortality here. But this exposure also conveys the knowledge of another dying that is inseparable from that experience of finitude. For these stirring, poignant lines strongly echo the scene from which we started: Blanchot's account of that being—a child, in this instance, standing before a garden in winter—who knows again, in the hiatus of an experience of the nothing, the death of the *infans*, that *passing* whose event (and the immemorial, furtive knowledge it brings) can never be brought entirely to speech, be it determining in its recessive return for the broken line of an entire existence. This other dying is an exposure which, for the subject that will have known it (be it a child, "seven or eight perhaps," or the adult who "lives later," and for whom this defines the experience of literature), is a *desistance*.[16]

The subject desists in meeting again that verge, that limit that was once traced at the very passage into language. But the site marked by the singular presence of phrase (from which the "I" has been displaced, or in reference to which it could not hold: a presence to no subject, in fact—*il y aura eu phrase*) is also the site of an opening. Phrase III will insist on this point when it returns to the difference between a child's experience of the onset of forgetting (and again we will have the mention of those few poor details: the light, the grass) and the possibility given to the adult of assuming the knowledge of the separation it brings—assuming its exposure and something that will be called the truth of this exposure. To approach this latter experience, however, we have to follow the way in which Lacoue-Labarthe introduces the shared relation to which I have referred.

Section 2 of Phrase II in fact recounts the onset of this relation shortly after offering the suggestion that the story (*l'histoire*) Lacoue-Labarthe seeks to recount, or recite ("unfortunately, perhaps, a kind of myth" [P, 13]), this story of renunciation, has transpired over a period of ten years. But immediately Lacoue-Labarthe removes this temporal indication from any historical frame, describing the environing circumstances of this narrative as a time of catastrophe where the contemporary is nothing but novelty (P, 13). Look and listen, he insists, if only to recognize that what truly happens, through us and beyond us, remains an enigma. The meaning of the epoch within which these ten years unfold thus remains withheld, and the dating offered is that of an event whose precise situation in temporal order is, strictly speaking, indeterminable. It is only from within this suspension that a belated beginning of a relation between the two protagonists announces itself and is declared in gestures and a night of "approximation": "the noise and the silence of voices, the limpid narrative of what we did not know of ourselves and persist in not knowing" (P, 14). "Approximation," then, or what we might call each literary expression on the verge of phrase: a *near saying.*

Thus "ten years ago," Lacoue-Labarthe tells us, something of this narrative sounded for someone (and is this other perhaps not first of all the one who has been cast into writing with the experience of desistance?[17]) as the echo of verses from Racine's *Andromache*:

> *(and that it should be a question of exile, of separation, of inadmissible renunciation, is in no way foreign to the matter; no more so than is the rejection, the enjambment):*
>
> . . . how will we bear,
> Lord, that so many seas separate me from you?
> That the day should begin again, and the day should end. . . . (P, 15)

Something sounded, he continues—phrase?—*between prayer and discourse* (P, 15). To which Lacoue-Labarthe then adds the crucial clarification that should renunciation ever be achieved, it would occur in prose, *oratio soluta*: an interrupted discourse: "*What would be today, I force deliberately, the text of distancing and dissolution. Broken, then, or fragmented, commensurate with the solitude* [. . .]" (P, 15).

Here, then, in this evocation of a fragmented discourse, we would have the textual condition of the saying, the sober diction/writing of phrase. Every word of this sequence ultimately calls for some commentary inasmuch as Lacoue-Labarthe summarily characterizes (but with stylistic effects that will also fall under the exigency of renunciation) the writing toward which *Phrase* strains to the extent that it seeks to bring to language the promise and the exigency of what echoed in the verses of Racine and Baudelaire. What is at stake, once again, is the renounced saying of phrase ("Let us admit, consequently, that it is necessary to learn to renounce, slowly; to no longer want to pronounce. Then there can be phrase" [P, 13]). But it is only once we define the full meaning of terms such as exile, interruption, and separation that we can begin to appreciate Lacoue-Labarthe's appeal (in the full epochal and existential senses) to a notion of fragmentation. Here, let us simply attend to Lacoue-Labarthe's insistence (his page makes the point twice) that the bringing to language of phrase would involve something echoing between prayer and discourse. Because what follows in the section of Phrase II we are reading is a relatively lengthy enumeration of discursive modes that are in some manner comparable to prayer, at least inasmuch as the latter carries the subject of such an enunciation into some form of pure address, perhaps even some effusion.[18] Presumably, phrase would run like a current, perhaps a scansion, beneath these "modulations," these expressions of a state of affliction which recall the supplication of the opening lines of the volume while also pointing forward to forms of "pure address" to come:

> *Imagine the body bent over the "it's nothing" of suffering or the "why?" without answer of affliction; imagine it failing, its breath caught, but speaking—murmuring. This is supplication.* (P, 16)

There follows, after a particularly powerful evocation of a form of struggle and agony in relation to what he names "the inexorable," the poor remainder of a fragile state: "*these few words that escape the throat*"—a demanding adoration ("*help me, love me*"), an imprecation. "*Pure, empty address*" (P, 16). Perhaps it is heard, he continues, even though it is "without relation": "*Why would we write otherwise?*" (P, 16).[19]

Indeed, writing would not occur had phrase not echoed in the "modulations" of plaint, supplication, demand, fury, love, etc. But how could this precarious, "delivering" enunciation be truly brought to sound (*from phrase*)—particularly in the joyful *Stimmung* of mourning, as it was thought by Hölderlin[20]—without the *writing* experience of renunciation? Phrase III has thus introduced, in its third section, a singular complication by juxtaposing the modalities of "effusion" in which phrase resounds with the stated imperative of a "renounced" discourse, which is the only form that could measure up to the separation known in the experience. We are summoned to hear the tones of lamentation, supplication, adoration, etc., that resound throughout this volume, *from the distance of its writing*. The difficulty of this exorbitant exigency will continue to gather as we follow this history of renunciation.

Phrase II is followed by a kind of note, a "Post-Scriptum" of a more theoretical, though still testimonial, cast that is no less crucial than what has preceded for introducing Lacoue-Labarthe's thought of phrase. It must also be followed carefully in that it helps set the terms of the *tragic* course of what will follow, though it would ultimately demand an essay of its own in that it explores the desistance known by the subject to which phrase comes as a kind of effraction. The address of phrase, we are told, issuing from nowhere and no one, brings a violent exposure to no ascribable origin. It is overwhelming, precisely as an exposure to no determinable source, even though its insistence, as we have seen, is defining for the self that never fully knows it:

> *And what I call "phrase" is thus what confronts me, what has always confronted me with what is not and cannot be, and in the face of which I am forever without relation. For this reason stricken at its touch, overcome, to the point that it is my very self that slips or stumbles, leaves or abandons itself, being reduced to almost nothing at the moment this comes upon me—which is to say, already no longer reaches me.* (P, 20)

These are in fact difficult pages by reason of the brutal frankness with which Lacoue-Labarthe describes the abjection of this desistance. It is, to put it gently, *not quite* or *no longer* Lacoue-Labarthe who hears its recurring refrain. And while it is liable to come in utterly banal, even squalid moments of bodily activity ("a sordid or obscene occupation, indifferent physiological preoccupations" [P, 21]), what it opens is "much worse" than what we might vaguely refer to as our animality: "*And much worse, in the unbearable, than joy. I find myself infirm, I lose myself there, unable to do anything about it*" (P, 21).

But these lines must be confronted, in their desperate attempt to say the loss of self, because the dying portrayed never wholly passes. The desistance is somehow progressive, in the manner of a malady; it is irremediable. He may well come back from each seizure, each disappropriating experience; in each case, he says, there has been a term to the agony. But the vital spring that allows this return inevitably weakens:

> *Hence the immense distraction, which is ever more accentuated. The distance that grows more severe in relation to everything. Indifference. I go silent: the phrase stiffens me—cold consumption—slowly. It takes my breath away or inhibits my respiration, asphyxiates me. Methodically, systematically, ages me. Ruins me, not to say more nobly: "engulfs" me. Ruins and harrows me because it is a weakening: deterioration.* (P, 21)

Here, in this accentuating, slowly driving dying, is the destructive underside of the experience of phrase, the mortifying grip of phrase that will doom the relation that he will not delay in evoking, immediately now, in exquisite terms. Like Hölderlin, Lacoue-Labarthe was a master in the alternation of tones.

The lines to which I refer are exquisite in the manner of a receding note of great beauty. And, indeed, it is in the form of such a recession that relation is first evoked here. Hesitating to refer to his suffering of phrase as a "passion," Lacoue-Labarthe is unable to deny the insistence of the term for his effort to reach that one who offers herself only in withdrawal—not in some reserve, but by an approach into nearness that is inescapably a distancing (*éloignement*), both temporal and physical. This is the first real appearance of the other who figures in this story of renunciation, though the face is in fact withheld ("eyes shut, the visage closed upon itself: this is not a visage, it is unrecognizable" [P, 21]). We will think immediately of Eurydice, though Lacoue-Labarthe will subsequently give another identification to this veiled one, naming her both lover and "*kère*" (a term he clarifies as referring to a goddess of death [P, 50]), while clearly linking this evocation to the loved one by toying with the addition of the letter *l*. But this identification, and the severity of the described refusal, should not mask the nature of Lacoue-Labarthe's response, which he once again compares to his relation to phrase:

> *It cannot but recall such a movement [the reference is again to the term "passion"], because in the one as in the other case—and sometimes they cannot be distinguished—there is given only what is already given (the parts already touched, the phrase already heard), without there ever being given what has given. But something, never a thing, withdraws or withholds itself, and nothing else happens or is even possible other than a desperate imitation of this ebbing.* (P, 21–22)[21]

The relation to phrase and to the other are thus, at moments, indistinguishable, and no following of their recession is possible other than an anxious, obsessional holding to what escapes ("Hence the prudent and minute attention, the ceremonial, the rites. Hence the fear [. . .]" [P, 22]). This is a music, a touch that is overwhelming, and yet distantly recognizable, distantly intimate. The touch *separates* and provokes to a desperate mimesis of almost nothing, an impossible step of accompaniment that Blanchot had named *pas*. This exercise of impossible fidelity in a mimesis without model is also what Lacoue-Labarthe sought to name literature. And we will understand from the withdrawal described here that renunciation, as Lacoue-Labarthe understood it, had to take form in what Blanchot had termed "an assent to refusal."

It is here that Lacoue-Labarthe declares that what he is attempting to understand is what he has read and reread in Hölderlin of the tragic *caesura*—that moment of "forgetting" where God and man separate in the extreme of passion. Where there has been caesura, we may assume, there has been phrase; it has come with the birth to a dying:

> In such a moment, man forgets, himself and the God, and turns around like a traitor, certainly in a saintly manner. At the extreme limit of passion, there subsists, in effect, nothing but the conditions of time and of space.
>
> At this limit, man forgets himself because he is entirely in the moment, the God because he is nothing but time; and either one is unfaithful, time, because in such a moment it veers categorically and beginning and end, in it, can no longer rhyme; man, because in this moment he has to follow the categorical turning about and thus, in what follows, is absolutely incapable of equalling the situation of the beginning. (P, 22–23)[22]

"Caesura" will name the separating event that marks the time outside all chronological order of this "history of renunciation."[23]

It is an event, once again, of an import no less ontological and destinal (in the sense Heidegger will forcefully give to it) than existential, even where it is lived in inescapably personal or "subjective" terms. Lacoue-Labarthe will not shy from the contamination between those categories philosophy would seek to distinguish: *Erfahrung* and *Erlebnis*.[24] But he will also not shy from the reference to the divine and what the "passing" of God (for Hölderlin, a categorical turning-about; for Nietzsche, a "death") means for the order of meaning itself—for from this turn, beginning and end can no longer "rhyme." And this too defines the meaning of renunciation (as well as terms such as "interruption" or "fragmentation") for Lacoue-Labarthe, who never ceased to accompany Hölderlin himself, even unto the very end.

THE EXIGENCY OF RENUNCIATION: EVENT AND RETURN

We are now prepared to read the story of renunciation in its full tragic configuration as the story of a shared disaster. It begins with "Two Examples" (the subtitle of Phrase III), the first of which distinguishes what is perhaps a child's primal experience (of an exposure to *nothing*) from what is known of it on the part of those who come later and await its return.

> The child, supposing it is him, looks. Or else,
> perhaps, has looked. What he sees nevertheless, what
> he saw,
> no one will ever know, not even he who will
> have forgotten it in advance, but will not cease to
> affirm having retained
> the immemorial memory: the arrival of nothing
> at this shore without edge. Sweetness and pain,
> together.

> It is only barely if there sometimes returns the
> memory, for example, of the dark passage in the grass
> of light. Or else of something else, unrelated.
> But who could retain the memory
> of a dazzling: of that faint failing
> when the faulting look sees what for it should not
> be seen?
>
> As for us, who were simply there, we waited.
> The black passage of the light was the same, or at
> least similar.
> It was necessary that we leave one another, but
> without reproach, because
> this distance, the passage and the lapse, we knew
> better than he, the child, we knew that there is no
> prohibition against
> suffering them, and that one can sink
> just as much in the height, the light:
> fall into the blue of the sky, pure effacement.
> (P, 25–26)

The echo of the "primal scene" from which we began is unmistakable, if only by virtue of the appeal to an act of supposition. In Blanchot's "scene," however, the appeal to supposition (made by an unidentifiable narrator) was made to those who live later, whereas in this account the narrating voice (who will apparently figure in a "we") supposes only that it is a child who is seeing or has seen. There is or has been a scene (of seeing), and it is supposed that this seeing might be attributed to a particular child—who could well be the child in the memory of one or both of the two (though the phrasing of the first sentence implicitly singularizes). These latter, in their turn, are said to *have been waiting* in a time that seems of necessity to be *after*, but indefinite in relation to the child's seeing; the forgetting from which they wait is without temporal determination. Indeed, the qualifying "simply there" appears to name a modality of existence that is to be distinguished from that of the posited scene with its supposed subject. This does not make the past event (which has passed, perhaps, without ever occurring in any lived present—hence its near presence) any less real, but suggests that its affective insistence ("sweetness and pain") has perhaps relayed the *requirement* of some fiction (e.g., that of the supposed child)—or a different fiction, in any case, from the one that constructs a "simple" existence.[25]

Again, in relation to the "primal" experience, only the scene is given as occurring/having occurred (but is the fact of seeing even certain, and is it even a scene?), while the subject of this scene is exposed to question. But once the latter question opens for us, we cannot but ask what of this event requires the figuration or identification. The text offers relatively little in this respect, for it is not entirely clear that the child and the one who claims to have retained an "immemorial" memory are in fact the same. Can it be the child who will in advance have forgotten what has been seen (forgetting then being the condition of the seeing, if not the "primal" phase of an occurrence that emerges only in a *nachträglich* fashion) in order to become the subject of this retention; and does he then join the "we" of the last section? Or is this survivor of the scene another? Their claim to an "immemorial" memory, in any case, is firm. Thus, in response to our last question regarding what *requires*, we might say simply that an immemorial claims, however faintly or indirectly its return is known by those or the one who are/is prompted retrospectively to assign a subject and some minimal "scene" to its early event. We know too (we who know what those who lived later knew "better") that this claim carried a charge of guilt regarding what is described explicitly as a transgression. The child was exposed to something interdicted, something that was not to be seen: "the arrival of nothing to this shore without edge." Such a vision, such a dying, which belongs to the very coming of the day (which is the lesson of both Hölderlin and Blanchot) falls afoul of, or at least escapes, every law and every bond, including, of course, the parental. Psychoanalysis will say that such knowledge must be repressed (and how, in any case, could it ever be held?). But how does it come to be that there is no transgression in suffering the return of the fall from the day (*défaillance*—this fall is a failing) and the separation in pure exposure to the blue of the sky? From whence the sovereign knowledge of this ecstasy, this falling, that carries Hölderlin's *lieblicher Bläue* into a Bataillan sky? And how does it lift this prohibition or reveal the innocent guilt to have been somehow in error? Of what is this separation without resentment an *example*?

The questions will only continue to multiply as we proceed to what is apparently the second "example" of Phrase II, a spare but beautiful evocation of an exchange of unattributable voices (presumably they belong to the protagonists) over three evenings of the same "endless blue." What these detached voices ("no one listened to them") require of one another or of what has sounded between them in this "incessant arrival of separation" cannot be known:

> I believe that these are incomprehensible things, over
> which no power is given to us. We
> are most often obliged to say: so it is. (P, 27)

With this acquiescence (already renunciation?), there remains only a note of voiceless supplication, the "heart of silence" of a distant rumor—what is left of the emptying recession of phrase.

What joins these two fragmentary accounts in which the narrating voice finds itself in some way separated from the experience it appears to have shared? Beyond the insistence of the blue and the modalities of separation it tinges, there is one common trait: acceptance. In the first "example," a peaceful separation is not without a kind of expiation or appeasement, perhaps even the recovery of an in-nocence (thus an infancy) a child could not know.[26] In the second, the acquiescence bears a fated character, though effacement does not spell ruin. There is perhaps even a hint of deliverance. The link is thus faint, but we may perhaps conclude that these two "examples" offer, minimally, the promise of renunciation, if not the promise renunciation will bring. The latter will come, however, in a succeeding evocation of the child's experience of the "immemorial" (the dying by which it comes to the day) in Phrase IV, and in the pages of Phrase VIII—two elegiac accounts of the sharing of a separating exposure which appear to prepare an effacement that might be described as the joyous face of desistance. Let us therefore turn to these two stunning poetic statements.

Phrase IV begins by recalling an experience of simplicity in a summer's retreat, an early chapter in this history of renunciation. But the ease of being together evoked here (graceful but also terrifying in the "transparency" of gestures and weighed upon by a "reserve of memory" and "something decided") cedes quickly, in the wave-like movement of this poem, to a mounting anguish and a repeated separation ("several times," as with the three nights of "Example 2" from Phrase III). Again, there is something like supplication in an almost pure note:

> It is possible, I know, that this is
> nothing other, fundamentally, than a barely
>   comparable moment: a song,
> a tenuous mode, each time,
> but just, of imploring:
> "Why must we be abandoned?" (P, 31)

Here, an acquiescence like that of the second "example" is urged, and acceptance that this moment is to be thought as what *holds* the possibility of simplicity, what gathers the near and familiar and what defines the inaccessible (the border is named after a path before which the two hesitate: "*la vie profonde*," this path is called [P, 32][27]). The note holds, then, but it also admits the building of a succeeding wave from the ground of the distress from which the questioning call ("Why must we . . .") emerged. This wave comes ("drawn from farther away in forgetting") in an "hour" of interruption that marks the recurrence of the caesura that first prepared this space of shared separation and exposure:

> because
> it is, always forgettable, always, drawn
> from further afar in forgetting, in what is secret,
> the hour in which
> this must be interrupted. A storm's light.
> And the breath, just barely. We know, it has been
> told to us:
> born out of breath, suffocating, committed
> to this return of the void in us, to this arrest from
> which comes
> fear. (P, 33)

Here, again, is an exposure like that attributed to the child in Phrase III, though it is now identified more immediately as a birth that is destined to return as a kind of dying in its recurrent interruption.

Significant citations would be required to convey Lacoue-Labarthe's manner of articulating this punctuating return with that of the onset of passion and its aftermath in another note of response to desolation, a sort of prayer.[28] The details of what appear to be a supervening time in Alsace are also precious for the broader narrative. But I will focus, at this point, merely on a recurring evocation of birth, and Lacoue-Labarthe's striking assertion that he *recognizes* this origin in the interruptions and suspensions of this largely idyllic passage. He knows, like a child (is this again the child of Phrase III, the child he perhaps was?), from whence the exposure comes, and he knows, like this child, what passage is required. He knows also a promise of redemption:

> Unknowable what
> arose there and made you vacillate,
> without words, bowed. But without tears, without
> dread.
> And in like manner the child, come evening, who
> caught the meaning:
> "Let us pass to the other bank" was not afraid. He
> knew,
> by no knowledge, he sensed,
> as I, at this table, this evening, under the usual
> lamp, I know, without knowing, I know
> that there still traverses us, trembles in us, the abject,
> the superb tremor from which we were born,
> disjoining us, endlessly, throwing us to the edge
> where it is henceforth barely
> we who shudder, having foundered well before,
> battered, for having come to the brightness
> of the day.—And if I am hurting or afraid, who will
> watch
> over me?—I will watch over.—And who will be able
> to hear me if
> I call?—I will, I will watch over, I will listen.
> —And when we will have made the step, one and
> the other?
> —Vast is the reserve of what has darkened. And we,
> we will always have
> known, we will have known it, that we were
> lesser. The same will be the earth and
> same the rain that will bathe our face. (P, 38–39)

One reassures, but both are in fact children or "lesser" and in some measure powerless (though another power is affirmed in the accomplishment of the "step," the passage to which they are enjoined in assumption of this destiny) in relation to what holds them and gives them the possibility of dwelling in time and on the earth until their passing, in what the narrator will call in the following lines "the just alternation of hours" (P, 39).

But let us pause here to ask somewhat insistently why a *child* has again been accorded the sense and the retention of the "immemorial" memory of a birth. Because we cannot simply presume that a relation to the birth in question is necessarily a child's privilege. Indeed, Blanchot made it clear that we must distinguish infancy (understood here as a condition of exposure) from childhood. His "primal scene" has a markedly belated character; it is attributed, by supposition, to a child who is already seven or eight. Nonetheless, Blanchot's few reflections on childhood suggest that children are close to infancy by reason of a susceptibility to fascination.[29] Lyotard, for his part, found in children a peculiar availability or vulnerability to the event and a marked perdurance of the "phrase-affect." Both of these treatments of childhood should be pursued, perhaps, in relation to the more general motif of the slow maturation of the human child, and at this point we might simply link to this motif the notion that children are for some time singularly open to some form of recurrence of that first "throw" into the day that is at once the opening of language and subjectivity and an experience of the abyss of experience ("nothing is what there is," wrote Blanchot, "and first of all nothing beyond"). Children, in other words, would be nearest that edge, that state of exposure that is infancy. And because they are capable of some knowledge or reflective retention of that infancy, they are our nearest relay and perhaps our surest reference for the presence of an ongoing sense of exposure. We have no concept of childhood, Hölderlin declared, even as he turned repeatedly to childhood to figure an origin.[30] We can perhaps only suppose, from the ground of an insisting recollection that we associate with our childhood (*our own*—though this attribution of property is obviously very precarious) that an experience of the kind of interruption Lacoue-Labarthe attributed to phrase recalls an "immemorial" already known.

Returning to the poem, might we not further presume from the scene of reflection presented (where an innocent knowledge is redoubled by the writer's later knowing, without knowledge) that it is by rejoining something of childhood/infancy that the destiny that has come upon the two might be assumed? It is an infantile knowing of the necessity of passage ("Let us pass to the other shore"—i.e., we must go forward from this bank onto which we have been thrown in our birth, in coming to the day) that prefigures and offers, to the narrator at least, the step that is to be made from a childlike anxiety and dependence into the reserve of forgetting that holds redemption. From the humility of an assumption of finitude, whose possibility is given in the passing of infancy (this is the "assent to refusal" described by Blanchot), the narrator can declare that the earth and the cleansing rain will be the *same* for us in our going down (to adopt, now, a phrase from Nietzsche).

"Not as I will, but as you command it of me," reads the line from Hölderlin cited as the epigraph of the section we have been reading, Phrase IV (P, 29). The acquiescence, as we see now, is prefigured for Lacoue-Labarthe in early childhood. It proceeds from a "primal" knowledge of exposure, as we read in Phrase III, but also what appears to be a stirring of a capacity for making the passage required by this elemental caesura that is our "birth" to the day. We asked earlier how this passage could be made without transgression, even if it proceeds from a seeing that represents a fault. We will be told now, in the last sequence of Phrase IV, and after a declaration that a *dwelling* is possible once "the step" has been made, that this possibility is given by obedience to, or rather love for (a love that is "against ourselves"), a *truth* whose redemptive coming is declared forever imminent. It is by a love, therefore, for the impossible advent of what has held this relation and whose "impossibility"—for it can never be held and is known as a kind of fate—is not suffered but assumed. (They will not have been its "victims," we are told [P, 40].) And it is by a limitless yes to all that comes in the time so prepared. The leap reminds us of Hölderlin's own ("may the Holy be my word"), even in the concluding note of sobriety:

> And everything that will come in this way, we accept
> it
> we say yes to this affliction, yes to indifference,
> yes to the things still to be born, to things dead,
> without relation to us,
> in decline and in the night,
> we say it, that there may thus come a time
> that it should come, when we will be the very
> appeasement of the earth
> and the transparent seasons
> of men, we will give our strength without measure,
> our language, without measure, and thought,
> we will consent to the immense forgetting,
> to the desolate realm, we will have this patience,
>
> the required firmness, we will have it, we will have
> to. (P, 40–41)

Il le faudra: it will be required. One cannot read these last words without recalling Lacoue-Labarthe's long-standing attention to the phrase *il faut*, whose imperative can also point to a wanting.[31] At the same time, readers familiar with Blanchot's *Death Sentence* cannot read this extraordinary page of affirmation without the chilling recognition that this has been, in significant measure, a citation.[32] Does this remove anything from what is said? Perhaps not. Perhaps not at all. But perhaps the very fact of citation introduces an anticipating note of the disaster to come. I will return below to the importance for Lacoue-Labarthe of this motif of citation.

Between Phrase IV, which we have just considered, and Phrase VIII, where phrase sounds again in a joyful mourning for those whose joining has been so overwhelmingly affirmed, there are in fact three segments with ominous implications. But let us return to them after turning to Phrase VIII, which articulates perhaps more powerfully than any other the form of meaning Lacoue-Labarthe gives to those modes of expression for which he employs metaphors of flowing from Phrase I forward. Phrase VIII, by ekphrasis (for it meditates on a statuette), follows the verses of Dvorzak's "Stabat Mater" to give voice to a shared lamentation. The lamentation, given in the Latin of Dvorzak's piece at the start of each section, is redoubled, in counterpoint, with a series of veiled allusions to a birth that could not come (P, 63, 64). It is then modulated again with sorrow and lamentation in relation to the birth to loss—or, more precisely, its return—on the part of those who have suffered this advent, this caesura that is the opening of the relation itself ("since dying brought us to birth" [P, 69]). The sequence as regards this last tragic experience is announced in terms that resonate with what is heard (again, the poem starts and ends with ekphrasis) in the holy mother's "lucid voice"—a call that announces a phrase, in the form of a kind of gentle sentence, for those joined in lamentation:

> Who, in me, will have heard it,
> the call, who, even before being able to hear it?
> I saw the day, its noises resounded, her voice
> lucid, tightly drawn, the rumor become
> phrase: a commandment, a kind of strict law

> dictated, yet without the least
> bitterness or the least hostility,
> like the gentlest of injunctions. (P, 65–66)

The call is not properly from the other with whom Lacoue-Labarthe shares this lamentation; indeed the verses suggest that it may be *of the day itself*. But we may assume that it comes via the other, phrasing what is "signified" in tears, as Section 5, which I cite almost in full, explains to us:

> The signification of tears
> is first that we are
> prey to time. Is first of all, in this cold,
> that we are expulsed. In this time.
> Yet "common to all
> is the impenetrable." But the sky, for itself
>
> is perfectly open, it is brilliant like
> metal, it blinds.
> The signification of tears is not, therefore,
>
> that a pain should cease, the desolation; nor
> that we should live in want of that more ancient
>   beating
> (the non-felt, nevertheless always there)
> but that, our eyes wide open, finally
> our sight should be withheld; there only, there
> is given to us "the extreme tension of pain
> and joy." Given to us
> to hear stir in us, in the constriction of the throat,
> the soft voice that we know is not our own. (P, 67–68)

I noted above that the term "caesura," as it is taken over from Hölderlin in this text, is perhaps most aptly applied to (or understood in relation to) the experience of the opening of the relationship in this "story of renunciation." But this latter event, as we have seen, is in itself an opening to recurrence of that primal "expulsion" or throw in and by which we come to the day, that immemorial event that is also, for the being exposed in this passage, the opening and closing of a knowledge of nothing (I refer again to Blanchot's words on the death of the *infans*). So it is that in this passage the Hölderlinian caesura seems to be given a broad sense even as it speaks to the experience of those suffering a blinding exposure to the sky (we will recall the sky of Example 1 of Phrase III) and the sovereign extreme of a pain conjoined with joy. Twice a blinding is evoked to name a suspension of a specular, reflexive capacity in representation, and perhaps the opening of a third eye with the *gift* of what is at once the sovereign affect (perhaps that acute joy Hölderlin found in mourning) and the birth of a voice—the voice of no one—from the *angustia* of the throat. We will see very shortly a similar emergence in "*l'émoi*" of Phrase V, where the birth/breath of a thought appears as an incipient saying of phrase. The suggestion that this still silent saying might be understood as another kind of birth (after the earlier references to a loss) apparently prompts a defensive "Do not say: this is ignominious," and then a reiteration that what speaks in this overwhelming, devastating, awesome, and empty silence is not *of us*. Again, it is something, like blood ("Yours"), that would be *said* ("signified") in an effusion comparable to the flow of tears that Hölderlin brought to speech in "In lovely blueness . . . ,"

> Crying means this
> outflowing, this pure empty
> transport: beginning and end never again in accord
> since dying brought us to birth.
> We, in forgetting; we
> in the most faithful infidelity. What man
> would not cry? (P, 69)

The signification of such crying, once again, would be nothing other than what is given in the interruption or separation of that transport Hölderlin once named the tragic metaphor.

I have already alluded to ominous notes, and I should not leave Phrase VIII without considering them. They indicate that the shared relation is marked by a division, even a dissension. Both protagonists are exposed in this relation—and this binds them—but the exposure of the one is "more like a wound" while that of the other is "more like an infirmity" that condemns him to expressions that are "declarations and near canticles" (P, 62). "What do you teach?" he continues:

> That fright comes first
> and ends by holding this voice that I speak.
> That dead, I will be, in consequence, your silence.
> That we are an insult: to the day and to the earth.
> (P, 62)

Hence perhaps the anticipated declaration of the "ignominy" that we have read.[33]

From whence has this division come? The text gives very little by way of elucidation, though it invites us to grasp its origin from Lacoue-Labarthe's experience of desistance. Let us move back to Phrase V now, which presents in dialogical form what Lacoue-Labarthe does not want to name a scene for the fact that it engages something that precedes any interpretative account or representation whatsoever and thus remains "secret" (though there is nothing secret), or better, *unavowable* for the subject that has desisted in this non-event. By this very form and through an insistent citation of Blanchot (this section, as I have noted, is also dedicated to Blanchot), Lacoue-Labarthe indicates that he is reading the late pages from *The Writing of the Disaster* as he recounts a singular experience of *suffering* the advent of phrase. The experience is not dissimilar to what Lacoue-Labarthe described in the opening paragraph of his "Post-Scriptum" in Phrase II, except inasmuch as it is presented as one of a wholly disappropriated speaking—the onset of an uncanny discursive flow, a fragmented elocution that is without voice and spoken by no one. The *défaillance*, the lapse from which this outpouring issues, indicates once again deterioration, degradation, weakening. But there is also, as I have noted, something on the order of a birth—the emergent breath and heartbeat of a thought as it passes into enunciation:

> *that ungraspable and seemingly inexistent moment removed from time, where, from the back of the throat,* thought *(what other word to use?) thus takes on a kind of intangible consistency—I would say, in all approximation,* takes a breath *and mingles with an expiration in which it is not lost but simply altered, and in being altered articulates itself or modulates itself in a vague, atonal song . . . punctuated more or less by the rhythm of respiration.* (P, 45)

We might await some further image of this birth, some figure, but it will not come. We are given something close to a pure arrival, the "pure address" evoked in Phrase II, though it will hang in suspension at its coming—neither aborted nor forming.[34] What then follows are Lacoue-Labarthe's "answers" in the dialogue of this section (the questions and hence any questioning instance are absent), and they move by complication and denial, removing from this saying any discursive substance and any discursive structure. What has been enunciated, it seems, are nothing but abstract, enigmatic phrases whose rigid order is only apparently grammatical and amounts ultimately to little more than parataxis. Nor does he allow that this could be conceived as a scene (*faite à quelqu'un*, one would say): "*No pain is dramatic*" (P, 47).

No further effigy, then, no "figure" beyond the evocation of a storm of discourse, "*the raging outside*" (P, 47). And what might have been promised as a birth was rather something on the order of a catharsis *without catharsis*:

> —No, this is not an image. In no way: the lapsing (the pouring out) is without effigy.
>
> *This is why, with the coming of the morning, in the feeble, blanched light of the dawn, everything seemed washed by that rain that had not fallen and had irrigated nothing. No storm had taken place.* (P, 47)

Or a catharsis, we might say, without relief or healing—a simple return to an immemorial dying that brings the ultimate condition of renunciation: limitless indifference. "*I could die*" (*Je pouvais mourir* [P, 47]). The statement is poised on the verge of an abyss, even two abysses. On the one side, the fatal deterioration Lacoue-Labarthe had described in his "Post-Scriptum" with only one possible end: letting oneself die (*se laisser mourir*); on the other, the opening of the possibility of a step, the renunciation of that day ordered by discourse and the letting come of another diction, another prose. *Je pouvais mourir* says both passivity and a capacity to let occur, indistinguishably. The true disaster is perhaps that Lacoue-Labarthe could not separate these as he fell.

With the "history of renunciation" guiding us, I will now hasten past Phrase VI, which gives Lacoue-Labarthe's speculation on the *kère* (here, the inclination to myth is perhaps most insistent and unsettling, even awkward[35]), and move to Phrase VII, which presents, in fragmentary and heavily veiled form, the first truly disconcerting signs of a foundering.

The tone is set partially in Phrase VII with citations from the version of Lamentations given in the Latin Vulgate in sections 4, 9, and 12. The cited fragments effectively strip the text of its reference to Jerusalem and leave the desperate plaint of a female voice. One cannot avoid noticing a reference to treachery that is very hard to reconcile with the "infidelity" affirmed by Hölderlin as the most faithful relation to the divine turning away. And one cannot avoid noting the juxtaposition of this lamentation with the troubled withdrawal of one who declares that the "immemorial" is unforgettable.[36] This is more than a withdrawal; the French gives *retranchement* (P, 55) to describe a retreat from human relations so severe as to suggest incapacity or sickness. This is the flight of a tracked animal (P, 56). Can we avoid the intimation here that Lacoue-Labarthe was overlaying Hölderlin's collapse on his own? However this may be, the renunciation in question, described as alternately childlike and guilt-ridden, appears to underscore the fatal dimension of separation—and thus what Lacoue-Labarthe terms (this must be cited in French) its *clair secret*:

> "Nothing will happen to me, nothing will happen to me." I believe that he had withdrawn, just withdrawn, and that having thus renounced, it was granted to him to admit the clear secret: separation.
>
> Don't forget that he had always said this, that he had even spoken of innocence ("the child with grey hair") and that, consequently, without ever wanting to, he could accept it, consent to it. [. . .]
>
> Others report that he moaned and lamented, "Oh no! Oh no! It's not possible," as though he ceaselessly recalled a fault, or faults. As though he wanted to efface his existence, disappear from this world, withdraw from the light of mortals (the living): "Because it is arid." (P, 56–57)[37]

And thus Lacoue-Labarthe's own admission in section 13:

> Because our time is measured out
> for ending and for turning away.
> Because it is arid. (P, 57)

The time outside time of this relation has effectively announced its closure; though like the beginning, the end delays in coming and is never definitive, let alone fulfilled.

Indeed, a passage of great beauty—an immense testimony of love—follows in Phrase IX, to which I will return. But the divergence just noted in the form of a juxtaposition (lament and an appeal to justice on her part versus flight on his) will nevertheless sharpen and take an increasingly identifiable form. Thus, Phrase XII:

> he seeks
> to make himself understood: he says he must leave, that he must
> give over; she, refuting, and refuting one by one his phrases
> with her intrepid voice (even in anger
> or in distress) demonstrates that they would perhaps be true
> if only he would not seek to retreat
> as, she had described, when in a storm and the din
> of water clarity and all distinct sounds are lost,
> there, now, ceaselessly. (P, 79)

In Phrase XX, we will encounter a comparable, but more severe, juxtaposition of flight and infirmity with an anxious but uncompromising demand for answers. In this last segment, the deterioration has advanced to a terrifying degree. The first two sections of it give testimony to an extreme separation from self, a disappropriation, disaggregation, and abjection that find a kind of echo, in turn, in the division of the other's voice, though here an acerbic demand (for answers, for justice) cohabits with a voice that is musical, disarmed, almost childlike. That the afflicted writer of this section can even hear the loving voice and recognize the grace of gesture is astounding, so great have the poisoning infirmity and the uncanny separation become. These are clearly dying notes, and yet the exposure somehow remains no matter how arid the relation has become.

But another note, another exigency, sounds from the divergence that I have perhaps too delicately evoked here.[38] In Phrase XII, her "refutations" become a demand for a just recognition of her presence and what speaks in her heart. This latter demand, however, even more strident and desperate in Phrase XX, is still not quite what we hear in the last verses of the same Phrase XII, where an unattributed voice calls for an unattainable probity in a citation from the Requiem Mass:

> I will sing Quidquid latet apparebit as no one
> Has ever sung it, in vain. And no one, believe me,
> no one
> Will have the uprightness required to hear it, ever.
> (P, 80)[39]

Was this apocalyptic tone latent in her apprehensive appeal to judgment, or was it called forth by his guilt and shame in such a way that it carries to an absolute what he hears in her judgments and demand for justice? Once again, though it follows a sequence of demands whose justice seems irrefutable (they are the demands of a lover who calls for what has been promised, and in sheer exposure), and then a more severe, more exposing challenge, the appeal to the *Quidquid latet apparebit* does not appear to be in her voice.

There had been already an appeal to justice in language in the idyllic period in Alsace evoked in Phrase IV.

> We had spoken of things
> still to be born and of those we thought

> would never again see the day. Of the precision
> of our language too, when it deplores or sets itself
> against the already said and against the unnamed.
> Of the wanting and of the just place of words. (P, 38)

But the struggle for truth named here, even the implicit judgment regarding a failing they inevitably shared (which will be repeated in Phrase XIX), does not point to "the storm of a sanction" (P, 81) or the absolute of the citation from the Requiem Mass. A different order of judgment has been sounded in that citation, just as it is a different meaning of justice that has been evoked. The latter, if not the former, points us toward the implicit condemnation that comes via "The Dead" in Phrase X. Here, an aged couple "without identifiable visage" present themselves as supplicants in search of a "semblance / of veridiction" in the "immense rumor" (P, 75). The haunting condemnation they bring is devastating. And what do they seek?

> not reparation, but justice
> quite simply, that one should carry out
> the laws known by all, the laws
> that govern our insignificance, affliction
> and our infirmity. [. . .]
>   We
> are the witnesses you deny in shame. (P, 76)

A reference to ashes in this poem, considered in light of Lacoue-Labarthe's deep preoccupation with the necessity of speaking to the fact of the Shoah, allows what is undoubtedly a just identification of this anonymous couple, but will probably not suffice. The haunting seems to speak more intimately. Do these two figures also call up, in ghostly return, what Lacoue-Labarthe had sensed before the path named *la vie profonde* (a site to which Phrase XI appears to revert on the succeeding page [P,

77])? His reserve forbids further speculation on this question and leaves us with the necessary anonymity of all those buried by the immense rumor of quotidian infidelity, an infinitely unjustifiable forgetting and denial.[10]

We will have heard, in any case, that the demand for a "veridiction" (certainly a rarity in modern French parlance and proceeding fairly directly from the Latin *veredictum*) has given the reference to law in phrase (heard already as a "sentence" or commandment) a new accent and, bearing on the "truth" of the relation, has also added a new dimension to the requirement of separation and thus to the imperative of withdrawal. A true diction, it seems, cannot be thought apart from an appeal to justice. Phrase XIX "(Prose)," returning to the theme of prose introduced in the first "clarification" and specifying the nature of an accomplished renunciation, states that only the dead are capable of this "almost unpronounceable" diction, though the "truth" of this diction is also what makes it humanly bearable. Here, the entire section must be cited if we are to appreciate the extremity of what is conveyed in what is a near conclusion of the history of renunciation, or the last stumbling steps toward a renunciation whose promise is held once again to an absolute: respect for the unpronounceable.

> I call prose a just diction, and, because it is
> just, almost unpronounceable. But indestructible.
> I read, in a translation of Eliot some months ago:
> "*And what the dead had no speech for, when living,*
> *They can tell you, being dead.*"
> Such, in effect, is diction.
>
> Just must be understood in the sense of justice,
> and consequently rectitude. Prose must not,
> in any instance lie or provoke humiliation
> or a distress without recourse. But this is not

sufficient: justness is the dictation of the true.
In other words: prose must enunciate a truth
that the dead, if they are just, would allow us to bear.
This is never something established. Only the dead who did not know what to say hold even the slightest authority.

The clinic where I am is clean, tidy, white. They are not too concerned
with me. I occupy, at the end of a hallway, a room that is almost bare, bright.
I take my meals with the other pensioners but I
hardly speak to them. They chat about everything and nothing,
watch one another, weave different kinds of bonds
amongst themselves (hardly of desire, certainly not of friendship
or love, but of jealousy), they speak ill of one another but in reality
speak only of themselves, pitifully.
Only a few, their glance always fixed, absent,
infinitely painful, never pronounce a word
except perhaps to beg for a cigarette or three francs for a coffee.
These, so close, are already
dead. Their elocution, barely audible,
is veridiction. It is in order to learn this mumbling
that I chose to come here, against myself
at the edge of menace and destruction,
in this abject solitude, between the tables
of the cafeteria, the trees of the park,
not to get hold of myself or renounce eloquence,
but in order to try to say as nearly as possible
what I must renounce:

> the bitter falsification, this evasive
> discourse, these remainders (or this excess) of "poetry"
> that have deteriorated our most just prose.
> (And I mean *our* prose, not that of the centuries:
> I am addressing myself to you, as you know.)
>
> A diction can well return to us, no reason
> to despair of it, if I make the effort
> to no longer trust the fury of words
> and if we are capable of respecting the unpronounce-
> able. (P, 113–115)

As much as one might want to find even a sliver of the saying that would proceed from this despairing search for the conditions of an accomplished renunciation—this attempted regression ("against himself") to the hither side of the false, the indirect, or "poetry": a retreat that is almost a fall—it seems all but impossible to catch anything beyond the indistinct murmur. Dissolution, solitude (Phrase II), yes, but without the announced approach of some form of return from the other side, some advent. What Lacoue-Labarthe may have gleaned from the brightness of his room in the clinic (which he describes, with astonishing irony, as "*claire*"), or from the dull murmur of the close dead, may or may not have exposed him to something of the unpronounceable. But from the liminal, minimal space demarcated in this text, there is no indication of an opening. The appeal to a possible diction merely echoes from a vain attempt to escape "the fury of words." ("If I make the effort," he writes—could this still be called "renunciation"?)

However, one striking theme emerges here that is especially worthy of note: the evocation of a *human* truth. The theme is not entirely new, for Phrase XVII, presenting Lacoue-Labarthe's struggle with religion, had evoked the ravages of instituted ritual and the "inextricable confusion of the religious and the political, that still purulent wound" (P, 103). The anger and hatred expressed with respect to the violations of religion speak in the name of a humiliated humanity. But with the citation of "Dies Irae" still ringing, it is difficult to grasp the grounds on which truth has come to be so humanly tempered. Or is this a protest, a kind of emerging counterpoint to a required, desired absolute for which Lacoue-Labarthe had yearned, at one point, as much as had the other? We must undoubtedly bear in mind here the haunting visit recounted in Phrase X by that couple "without identifiable visage" who seek "veridiction" and the justice ensured by "the laws / that govern our insignificance, affliction / and our infirmity" (P, 76). Antigone had appealed to laws of such an order in her own appeal to the dead (in Hölderlin's translation: "Who knows, there reigns below perhaps a different usage"[41]). Is it possibly from here, from this *other usage*, that Lacoue-Labarthe envisioned a more human diction? Did he seek, in joining the "ruined men" of the clinic, to gain the capacity to speak with and for the dead, and thus humanity?

Working from this last hypothesis, we might understand the true end of the history of renunciation (the end sought in the retreat to the clinic) to be an experience of finitude rejoining the one described by Blanchot in his efforts to define access to a "general" human experience in suffering, fear, affliction, and infirmity. And we will understand perhaps a bit better why Lacoue-Labarthe was so stunned by Blanchot's very last publication, *The Instant of My Death*, where mortal exposure opens the narrator to "suffering humanity."[42] Lacoue-Labarthe perhaps only glimpsed that other usage in his prose, the diction that would honor the human relation, but it sounded there to some degree in his very need for it.

But the scene in the clinic (from Phrase XIX) may also be read as an end or closing for the history of renunciation inasmuch as it offers the last apparent step in the struggle to renounce, giving way to no further saying and no further word of the relation that was at its heart beyond the mildest allusion. It marks a kind of zero-point from which there is no return. In Phrase XX, which occupies an uncertain place in the temporal sequence of the narrative,[43] there is an address to the other (words of love and admiration to which I have referred earlier) that issues from a place of utter disappropriation, utter ruin. There follow, in section 4, fragments that Lacoue-Labarthe claims not to have had the strength to discard, following his normal practice. Several of these, admittedly, are of extraordinary force; but they appear at this point as fragments, *épaves*, that have survived by some inexplicable contingency, mere remainders. It is not at all clear that these are somehow to be taken as instances of the fragmented discourse for which he had called, in Phrase II, many years earlier, in envisioning an interrupted or fragmented discourse. In Phrase XXI, the last, there will be hardly a mention of the relation that was at the heart of the history of renunciation, hardly more than a kind of admission (of admiration, once again), *after* separation.[44] I will return to the form of abandon described in this last section. But before approaching it and one last instance of renunciation from *Phrase* that I would like to offer in conclusion, in fond remembrance of a friendship (it opens upon the origin, the infancy so desired by Lacoue-Labarthe), I will shift modes, interrupting the account of the history of renunciation for a summative consideration of what renunciation meant for him. I hope, by this means, to draw threads of the preceding account together and thus prepare for a presentation of what was perhaps Lacoue-Labarthe's *nearest* annunciation of phrase.

RENUNCIATION AND SURVIVAL

"*to no longer want to pronounce*"

Heidegger's account of the poet's relation to language, with which Lacoue-Labarthe was intimately familiar, had pointed to the necessity of the poet's abdication vis-à-vis any naming pretention for the sake of a saying that would resonate with the enjoining grant of language. Here was the basis of the poet's *Aufgabe* (task; but in the German there also echoes *aufgeben*, to give up or surrender), prepared in an *Absagen* (a withdrawal or declining), a *Verzicht* (abandonment or resignation: the root *ziehen* is "the same word," Heidegger says, as the Latin *dicere* and the Greek *deiknumi*) and an *Entsagen* (resignation or abdication), each of which would already engage in some manner the saying to which they would open.[45] ("'Renounce' meant: announce, enunciate. 'Phrase,' in Greek, says roughly the same thing" [P, 13]). Lacoue-Labarthe was clearly envisioning something comparable. But in Lacoue-Labarthe's renunciation of a will to *pronounce*, we may also hear a slightly different intonation, one that bears on the subject's sovereign prerogative in matters of judgment (its capacity to pronounce), be this with respect to truth, or what is deemed to be right. Lacoue-Labarthe's struggle with the latter exigency had been painfully visible in his relation to Heidegger himself,[46] and it echoes even in his last work. *Phrase*, of course, represented a direct affront to any arrogation of the principle of reason in matters of judgment, demanding a different hearing and the learning of a different saying.

It must be added that the abdication of the prerogative of the subject in relation to an "order of meaning" meant more than an exercise of delimitation in relation to the millennial hold of Western metaphysics (whose grip Lacoue-Labarthe recognized with the utmost seriousness in all areas, starting with the political). It meant interruption and passage, an assumption of what modern thought, art, and literature had revealed of an interruption in the symbolic order (hence an opening to the exigency of fragmentation) and the abandonment of every temporal comfort in the form of some teleological ordering: beginning and end could no longer rhyme. To the experience of finitude implied by the "categorical" veering suffered by modern humanity, and still very much with Hölderlin (though exceeding him in severity), Lacoue-Labarthe also joined the exigency of renouncing every instituted religious reference. Again, the assault extended well beyond the critique of onto-theology; Lacoue-Labarthe required a categorical refusal of the almost immemorial evocation of holy names. That this required renunciation should fold back upon elements of *Phrase* itself and its insistent evocation of Christian themes—however stripped of their Biblical context—was surely recognized, in however conflicted a manner, by Lacoue-Labarthe himself, even if he was obscurely seeking another language for the sacred, as he was for justice itself.[47]

And to develop this last point more generally: would an assumed suspension of the will to pronounce not have required an added vigilance in an important part of Lacoue-Labarthe's later discursive stance in matters of history, art, religion, and politics? Readers of his critical work will be familiar with both an insistent and masterful rhetorical appeal to discursive authority (with frequent recourse by citation and allusion to names of distinctive weight) and increasingly subsuming or summative (sometimes reductive, in the view of this reader) conceptual and historical statements. The imperatives of probity and sobriety could easily be served and claimed by this exigent style which sought to answer to and bring forth an almost absolute critical exigency in matters of intellectual, literary, and political history. And perhaps this style was not ultimately incompatible with a different form of diction (if we give its place to fragmentation). But the line between upholding critical rigor and claiming critical or writerly authority proved a difficult one to negotiate for Lacoue-Labarthe—which is in fact one reason why *Phrase*, in its very deconstructive import, is such a valuable and important book in his oeuvre. Lacoue-Labarthe's own spectacular statement on the question of literary authority in "*L'agonie de la religion*" (one of the most just summations available on Blanchot's own relation to authority[48]) shows both an acute awareness of what was at stake, and his own struggle with the will to pronounce.

"How had he come to will the interruption of the discourse?"

The year 1969 saw the publication of Blanchot's *The Infinite Conversation*, a volume of immense scope encompassing critical essays on Bataille, Levinas, and Nietzsche, among many others; works of reflective thought (these include passages on *le neutre*, the narrative voice, and fragmentation); and a series of meditative dialogues reflecting back upon an opening narrative that presented in fragmented form a conversation and the aftermath of its breaking.[49] The dialogue moved through the peripeties of a relation between two aged friends whose suffering of a shared fatigue had an inexorable character by reason of "a word, a phrase" that had come between them. The phrase, which is apparently transcribed in the course of the exchange in the form of a peculiarly neutral sentence, could not be properly assigned to either, in the sense that either might say in a moment of liminal exposure that they *had been* this phrase in some singular manner. Thus it is not at all a matter of pointing here to some simple citation or repetition in Lacoue-Labarthe's possible re-engagement of Blanchot's text. But the saying of this phrase in Blanchot's text implied a difficult separation for the two interlocutors (a motif also visible in the closing page of *Le pas au-delà*) and the advent of another form of speech, a language of interruption. The history of separation in this dialogue was the history of bringing this other speech to language, much in the manner of the history of renunciation.

Desistance, for Lacoue-Labarthe, implied such a notion of separation. Most immediately, in the sphere of the personal (that is to say, beyond the "essential" separating—*é-loignement*—that occurred in the very contraction of the relation), this was separation from his partner. But, determining the exigency of this latter parting, it was first of all a separation from self in the form of a lapsing, or failing—a *défaillance* that brought fatigue, powerlessness, and, at its limit, an indifference, whose advancement Lacoue-Labarthe named deterioration. Desistance, as we have seen, followed the path of an ever more disappropriating infirmity, so disappropriating, in fact, that Lacoue-Labarthe came to feel himself occupied by malignant forces. "Phrase" had a debilitating effect and seemed to release a horrific form of becoming other, even an uncanny occupation. But we have also followed, in Lacoue-Labarthe's account of a night of catharsis (dedicated to Blanchot, as we will recall), the emergence of another indifference. Perhaps inseparable from the other weakness, it nevertheless had a *releasing* character. Hence the ambiguity of "*je pouvais mourir*," which I have read as his affirmation of the possibility of following Blanchot in what he called "effacement" or "exception." Lacoue-Labarthe had reached the point of being willing to renounce the order of discourse itself.

Je pouvais mourir—the phrase expresses an extreme of exhaustion, but also a strange capacity to assume interruption or separation, both from oneself and from the other ("we are held to it, constrained to it, as to / the irrevocable, which, the one forever following / the other separates us, the one apart from the other binds us" [P, 9]). The same extremity of exposure gave the possibility of hearing lamentation or prayer, and the possibility of knowing a joy in mourning. It gave even the capacity to recognize and affirm, in some moments at least, that effacement will overtake everything temporal. Blanchot had articulated this knowledge in the most lapidary form in his extraordinary memorial text for Bataille: "*Tout doit s'effacer*" (a simple but charged phrase that "everything must fade" can barely render).[50] Blanchot went farther than Lacoue-Labarthe in thinking what delivers in this movement, I believe.[51] But *writing*, as each author conceived it, would not have been possible without this other, affirmative turn in/from what Lacoue-

Labarthe named indifference, and I will conclude this volume by entertaining a passage that is not unrelated to the transport to which I have been alluding. Separation, in its epochal import (giving us themes such as "the end of metaphysics," "the death of God," or "a change in times"), or in its personal or interpersonal ones, held an abyss for Lacoue-Labarthe that no tragic thought could overcome. But renunciation also indicated a path if not beyond, at least through, the agon and the agony, and toward a possible writing of phrase.

"But this is a citation!"

The history of renunciation was conceived, as we have seen, as a gradual bringing to language of phrase in what Lacoue-Labarthe designated as prose. Initially described in Phrase II (dated 1979) as a fragmented, interrupted discourse, this prose was increasingly defined, as we have seen, with reference to the true and the just (hence a "veridiction"). This last development brought a renewed pressure to any recourse to the "poetic" inasmuch as this term marked by shorthand everything that might manifest some form of indulgence or posturing, be this in some subjective pathos or lyricism, or in linguistic expression. Few philosophers have had a more acute ear for the poetic or a better understanding of what both Hölderlin and Heidegger meant with the phrase "poetically man dwells." And few literary thinkers, after Bataille, have been as resistant to any form of poetic indirection or falsity. In the abject solitude of the clinic, we recall, Lacoue-Labarthe sought

> to try to say as nearly as possible
> what I must renounce:
> the bitter falsification, this evasive
> discourse, these remainders (or this excess) of "poetry"
> that have deteriorated our most just prose. (P, 114)

Would this not mean, to begin, leaving the protections afforded by the precious or even the overly precise, the defenses of syntax itself ? (No small matter for one I once named a "*syntaxier*," with an eye to Mallarmé and intending the highest praise.[52]) More broadly, what had to be unlearned were any habits of flight or any too easy recourse to the "poetic" gesture in the gradual process of finding the hold of another rhythm.[53] And ultimately it meant a renunciation of the poetic figure itself.

The latter purging of discursive indirection entailed a struggle with every form of citation or repetition. The history of renunciation, we will recall, threatened to be a recitation of *myth*; but it was haunted perhaps more intimately by the binding of citation. The posthumous volume on Blanchot reveals to what extent this had become a preoccupation for Lacoue-Labarthe in his last years.[54] But *Phrase* itself overtly stages this struggle for us in Phrase XVII "(Scene)" with a re-presentation of his own aging as the history of a struggle with a voice that has provided him with the equivalent of a script. Here, the question of citation rejoins that other "demon" that tormented and inspired Lacoue-Labarthe, that of mimesis. The persona who appears onstage, initially a boy of "ten, at most eleven," then an increasingly older "Lacoue-Labarthe,"[55] claims to "represent" no one, but will speak only what another has given him to say. He will not speak in his own voice or name, at least until the very end: "Do not forget that I do not speak in my own name" (P, 101).

Who has thus instructed this speech, this rendition of long reflections on the nature of thought, the passing of the gods, and the meaning of the categorical turning by which modern humanity was left exposed to a God who is "nothing but time"? Surely all of the figures to which I have pointed in these pages speak in this prompting voice (and we might want to add Artaud or Nancy). They are even joined by "Lacoue-Labarthe" himself, given the distinctive use of Hölderlinian categories.

And presumably it is "Lacoue-Labarthe" who brings the objections and increasing exasperation vis-à-vis any compromise with religion, the growing sense of revolt ("I feel mounting a nameless anger" [P, 107]). The motif of anger became, as we know from Lacoue-Labarthe's late publications, a core theme in his reflection on the "primal scenes" of Western literature, thought, and political practice.[56] But can one ever locate precisely the emergence of Lacoue-Labarthe's "own" voice in the last paragraphs of this scenic presentation—even if it is hard to imagine a more pure expression of Lacoue-Labarthe's anger and most extreme tragic thought than in the last words of impatience with the knowledge/the categories/the practices given us by our languages to think our finitude, and from which no thought is ultimately separable (even as it indicates the inadequacy of these "viatica")? Is it indeed Lacoue-Labarthe "himself" who retreats at the end into the persona of a humble but dignified actor who is little more than a functionary?

> But here I've gotten carried away. Please excuse me.
>
> *(He is silent for a long moment, straightens himself up a bit.)*
>
> In sum, I refuse to say "Amen." Or: "It's nothing, I expected this; I can accept it."
>
> There, that's it. I hope I've more or less properly fulfilled my task. I'm not at all sure: it was both too simple and too difficult. Inopportune, as well. But we don't get a second go.
>
> (The light goes out.) (P, 108)

I do not catch a citation in these last sentences (I'm sure I should), but I cannot but hear in the gesture a resonance of Hölderlin's: "For this is the tragic to us: that, packed up in some container, we very quietly move away from the realm of the living, [and] not that—consumed in flames—we expiate the flames which we could not tame."[57] Lacoue-Labarthe was quoted as saying, near his end, and with a beautiful self-irony, that he had perhaps imitated Hölderlin a little too much. But the troubled retreat from the stage we have read is perhaps still to be understood as a figure of exit from a life in citations.

Could any escape from mimesis (in this case, as citation) be envisioned? Translating Lacoue-Labarthe once, I found myself stumbling over a sentence whose meaning resisted me. The problem emerged fairly quickly from our conversation (it turned out that I simply hadn't been able to believe that Lacoue-Labarthe would want to say what it was saying) and I concluded with a smile. "So you believe that an escape from mimesis is possible? For the first time, I see a real divergence between us." The history of that divergence is hidden from me (I believe it eventually closed with respect to that early question inasmuch as I found my own path to interruption—one not dissimilar to the one Lacoue-Labarthe followed in a reading of Paul Celan's "Meridian" address in *La poésie comme expérience*); but I do not doubt that Lacoue-Labarthe saw in renunciation a path to a more frank prose.

"at the border of an accepted silence"

There is, as I have noted, a final step of renunciation in *Phrase* that is perhaps already no longer part of the "history" we have followed. Lacoue-Labarthe gives voice to this form of renunciation in Phrase XXI when he "clarifies" for a second time (Phrase XXI takes again the subtitle of Phrase II: "(Clarification)") his experience of phrase. Here, phrase presents itself as an unidentifiable but imminent or "possible" language that requires translation once the one writing stills the desire to speak and to intend to say something and allows the "fright of silence" its due in "all the noises of the outside" (P, 129). There is a form of struggle suggested, for this forever prior speaking that is to be translated is said to render foreign every language, beginning with one's own (the recognition of one's own voice in relation to this phrase is recognized as no less problematic). But the struggle—there is still "an imperious need to translate it. / Everything is lacking . . ." (P, 130)—does not seem part of the preceding, increasingly desperate effort, or even its abandonment. Whatever struggle there is appears, and by the very tone of this statement written in an unsituated present ("When I undertake to write it, this, when / I no longer speak" [P, 129]), to *come after*. Renunciation, at this point, is apparently what Lacoue-Labarthe has been *left* with, not something reached or *achieved*, as I tried to formulate this earlier, and it is said to bear upon the writer's relation to his language and his voice, neither of which he can now claim to recognize as his own. Renunciation is thus closer, here, to an acceptance of defeat, an acquiescence without affirmation, than to an attained mode of phrasing. Of course, Lacoue-Labarthe had sought to evoke the meaning of phrase in Phrase II with reference to an acceptance: "*For example a destiny, or a fatality*" (P, 13); but he also followed with a description of what an "accomplished" renunciation might bring (P, 15), namely a discourse of fragmentation. Here, in Phrase XXI, the phrase that would sound in translation comes only in "a song / that at rare moments we are given, perhaps, to hear / but that nothing would have permitted us to produce" (P, 131). Never could it be claimed as one's own:

> It comes from too far away, too many passions have composed it

and decomposed it, too many throats have intoned
it or cried it out,
it was too much the rumor of centuries, or too much
our origin. (P, 131)

In short, the effort to render phrase now underscores a fundamental anonymity, and Phrase XXI can be heard as describing a release from the struggle, the agon, that marked the history of renunciation as the history of a struggle with a singular destiny. The abandonment of the proper, however, does not suspend all recognition, for there remains the gift of the other's voice: "this flows from the source, I have nothing to deny" (P, 130). In this last, limpid "clarification"—understood, here, in the sense of a recovery of the pure clarity of the source—flow the names of this history of renunciation.[58]

Once again, there has remained in Phrase XXI the imperative of translation and a receptivity to the voice of the other, thus a vestige of the relation, but the overwhelming experience of a throw and the need to bring to language its signification (what Hölderlin conceived as the tragic metaphor) in a singular articulation is no longer present. The history of a renunciation has already ended. So, how, then, are we to think that latter end? I have attempted to indicate the difficulty by quoting at length from Phrase XIX, dated December 1999–March 2000. From the space of that text (the clinic), as we have seen, it is hard to fathom the faint sound that would accompany the coming eclipse. But a kind of end, or *surviving* end without end, had in fact already been announced or glimpsed earlier in the text. And I am even tempted to say that it had been announced twice, once in renunciation, once in acquiescence. From this perspective, we could perhaps understand the end of this history of renunciation, at least as Lacoue-Labarthe was capable of conceiving it, as something spanned and prolonged—as a suspended passage linking infancy and a still more enigmatic experience of that threshold that figures in poetic experience. Phrase IX describes a gift at the very limit of renunciation, while Phrase XIV, an extraordinary "example" of achieved acquiescence (here the "*c'est ainsi*" of Phrase III is translated with Beethoven's "Muss es sein?—Es muss sein"), speaks to a convalescence and then evokes a joyous, almost giddy experience of an arrest in time that is briefly given to us to hold:

> and that end
> which never ends, it must be perpetuated
> still a little, very little, just as is allowed to us. (P, 93)

I propose, therefore, to seek an end to the history of renunciation that had been seen before the unsituatable, final darkening by seeking a passage between these two experiences of a given time (from IX, then, to XIV). There is perhaps no definable, "real" end to the history of renunciation. Phrase XIX could be taken to suggest that it had also an abyssal, endless nature (in a very forbidding sense), despite its insistent call for a just prose. But an experience beyond this abyss had been offered.

A Late Return

I turn first to the poignant meditation in Phrase IX where Lacoue-Labarthe evokes, via a "transcription" of remarks by Wittgenstein, Mautner, Adorno, and Benjamin, the impossibility of translating in any speech the "inexpressible": here, his exposure to phrase, and, indistinguishably, to the other in their earthly, yet brilliant presence. (The contrast here with Phrase XXI, which also treats of the question of translation, is quite striking.) Writing, he explains, can perhaps capture, in its rhythm—if one waits, and this too involves something related to the "stilling" we have just considered from Phrase XXI—this wrenching experience of separation and *passing*.[59] The movement is one of expulsion or being carried *there*: in this instance to be expelled or carried to that place (*là*) where he is exposed to that one or that "thing" (*ce qui—celui qui*) who/that sustains him as "I who do not cease dying." Or it is to be carried to that place where "we know what *passing* is" (P, 72). But before the other of this history, in their presence, there is only the rarest speech. Lacoue-Labarthe's explanation of this concludes as follows:

> *We know each other more than I know myself. (Perhaps you will thus understand that I am never able to speak to myself, even less look at myself. I see everything blindly. But this strange blindness ceases with you. But this additional clarity, as though another degree were reached, is precisely what commits me to silence. Or at least to a rare speech. Speaking says always more than we are capable of, more than we are able to hear ourselves say.)* (P, 73)

With an intervening textual break, Lacoue-Labarthe then declares that only the address of prayer (almost indirect, so open is its address) gives the possibility of such speech before the face of the other. The indirectness obliged by this immeasurable nearness is then further underscored as Lacoue-Labarthe passes to remark in the next sentence that he can recall only a few rare verses (the word "rare" now recurs) outside Racine and Baudelaire, and he provides us with the following from Rimbaud's "Mémoire":

> Madam stands too straight in the field
> nearby where the filaments from the work snow
> down . . .
> Or:
> Plaything of that eye of dull water, I cannot grasp,
> oh! motionless boat! oh! these arms too short! either
> the one

> or the other flower: neither the yellow calling to me, there; nor the blue, friend to the ash-colored water. (P, 74)[60]

Is this recitation, too, a form of prayer, or would prayer bear the saying of the loss to which these lines testify? The lines from Rimbaud, in any case, have been spoken in renunciation, for what he rehearses in these lines, as he proceeds to indicate, is the passing of his own infancy. The lines are thus followed by a declaration that sets a term or a virtual barrier, which is none other than the barrier of finitude itself, as Hölderlin had defined it. There is no reversing the closure that occurs with this expulsion into time:

> *There is my infancy, what has ended, absolutely ended.* (P, 74)

And yet no sooner is this last, decisive, renunciation pronounced, than the barrier gives way to a return of a pure experience of a kind of caesura:

> *This morning, nevertheless, when you were near the pond—but neither "too erect" nor "holding yourself," even though "in the meadow" (at the foot of the tree, struck down, crying)—it was again, it was no longer, it was infancy. I was mute:* infans. *Sometimes, it is comprehension that takes our breath and our speech.* (P, 74)

The acceptance of an irreversible passing and what has been lost to it has effectively given way to an understanding of the signification of the other's tears in "pure, empty transport." The comprehension itself interrupts, allowing a return that is like an unforeseeable gift at the limit of the silence Lacoue-Labarthe has accepted in the presence of the other. Here, the interruption of the end brings the sudden return of a surviving infancy.

Of course, the history of renunciation evolves in its recounting in *Phrase* (that recounting has its own history, as indicated by the dates in each section), which makes the sense of an ending all the more difficult to define. Under the name of veridiction, as we have seen, Lacoue-Labarthe had gradually come to seek a prose more observant of the human. But the sur-passing return we have just read was perhaps as far as he could go in that part of the history that engaged the relation to the other. It offered what might appear as a final step for him—even if it came only as an unexpected gift, a pure exposure to the exposure ("the signification of tears") of the other in a form of deliverance in and from time.[61]

I write "in and from time" inasmuch as Lacoue-Labarthe's experience of the caesura is repeatedly offered to us as delivering into an irreversible time; it repeats an "immemorial" attributed to infancy, a "primal" exposure to nothing, as we have seen, but it is exile into an irreversible "separation" (from every origin) where "beginning and end no longer rhyme." Here, in the passage we have just read from *Phrase*—and after a rhyming quatrain!—an end is given as return to an origin that had been declared irrevocably lost. Of course, the "origin" itself, in this suspended time, is offered via the evocation of a poignant separation and a divided longing (with the yellow of something like desire, and the blue tending to the ashen darkness of something like death), the suspension conveyed in immobility and a child's powerlessness. But what is given remains the desired other shore, the other side of the barrier that forms in our experience of time. We must surely read this experience as a joyous end. And perhaps, in this suspended division, a return to the very articulation of something like phrase is occurring. But, it is crucial to note that if such an articulation is happening, this is occurring in a joyous recovery of *proximity*. The other has here captured the very existence of this infant being in a mute rapture. The child's *existence* is captured, not just his attention: this is more than a spectacle.[62] Of course, it is said to be, remarkably, understanding ("comprehension") that delivers to a pure, infantile existence in this manner—perhaps a poetic understanding. But this is an understanding of existence with another, toward another. I am wary of identifying this other too quickly in the terms of Lacoue-Labarthe's mythic construction of "three women, / in the courtyard of a farm" (P, 17)—though all three are conceivably here in this infantile exposure to a lost maternal presence. I prefer simply to stress that phrase, if it can indeed be conceived as emerging in this longing articulation of the yellow and the blue, is here finding its articulation in a scene of accompaniment, at the very limit of what Lacoue-Labarthe named *the maternal closure*.[63] Infancy finally figures here as exposure with/to another, despite the terrible solitude that will later come in experience of the phrase that must have echoed in the verses from Rimbaud (just as phrase echoed earlier with verses from Racine [P, 15]).

A desired end may have been given, then, in this last, furtive opening to something beyond the dying (perhaps the drowning) that also appeared with this return of the receding origin. As we have seen, the latter path, however tempting in moments ("*se laisser mourir*"), was, in turn, inseparable from that of "the irrevocable," a locution to which I again join "the irremediable" (that from which there is no convalescence). But the opening or access to the other that occurs with the return of the receding origin we have just read must somehow have always been there as a promise, despite the near presence of that other path evoked, perhaps, in the "ash-colored water." *Why would he have written otherwise?* And if we couple this opening to what we read in Phrase IV of the child's innocent knowledge of the impetus and necessity of passing over, we may have a glimpse of what Lacoue-Labarthe was seeking in his return to poetic origins.

Something of this passage is in fact given in Phrase XIV, that magnificent poem which moves through meditations on Eliot (particularly the *Four Quartets*), Conrad, Hölderlin, and Beethoven, to present passing-over initially in an "infernal" guise (where the passage over Styx finds its figuration in the land of the "disaffected"—the scene is San Francisco), and then, after an encounter with a passerby on a street that recalls to him the nobility of Antigone,[64] and previous passings-over (two near-death experiences), in a memory (via Rousseau) of something comparable to a rebirth.

> I knew that it had happened to me before
> to know that I had died. Twice over. About the first time
> there is nothing I can say. As for the second, I think
> it is not something of which I am prevented from talking: it was
> just the easy crossing over a path
> not very deep nor very broad, a coming and going
> at best between two shores of which one is in fact endlessly
> out of reach. But in the look that appeared and was exchanged
>
> there was, yes, "the feeling of my light existence." (P, 86–87)[65]

I will not try to add significantly to what Bailly has offered in a moving commentary on these verses, nor will I return to his development of the references to Beethoven's String Quartet no. 15 in this poem, beyond noting the vital mention that the mode of this piece was indicated by Beethoven with the phrase,

"Heiliger Dankgesang eines Genesenen an die Gottheit, in der lydischen Tonart" (A holy song of thanks by a convalescent to the divinity, in the Lydian mode). I will merely try to underscore Lacoue-Labarthe's manner of grasping the extremity of the passage through affliction that Beethoven captures in this song cast in a mode proper to pain and mourning, for he is apparently called back again to the entry into a self-effacing night "all of marble" that he described in Phrase III (P, 27), though the latter was a night of separation in the company of the lover and has become now one of a death in the soul (P, 84), a night all the more empty for the experience of abandon without recourse (P, 90). The song, as Lacoue-Labarthe refers to it in recalling his memory of its power for him in September 1983 (this is the time of Eugenio Donato's passing), "seems to pass on, if / one can use the word this way, beyond all memory" (P, 90). It thus *bridges* with the immemorial and *suspends infinitely* the experience of mortality in this slow crossing (one of many crossings in this poem of rivers), though it already requires, in the very silence of this transition, the refusal, the renunciation (!) of abandonment itself and the welcoming of the unexpected turn, the final declaration:

> But no is what must be said, no to the unacceptable
> calm, no to the dizziness, for as to this expiring
> slowness
> before the crossing, as it dies away, there's no doubt
> the suspense is finally calculated, just on the
> threshold
> of the ultimate declaration that returns from afar.
> (P, 90)

Section 4 of Phrase XIV will then go on to evoke the suspension of an ending in a way that gives it as perhaps something less than heroic, in the classical sense, or for which heroism cannot be adequate ("there is the tragic for us . . ."): "The hard thing, about a day that reaches its end, is / to accept that it doesn't end" (P, 92). Acquiescence will here involve forgiveness (letting go, perhaps), and learning: "But prosody had to be learnt in / Oakland from the man with blood in his name" (P, 92). The prosody of guitar music, no less![66] But the returning upheaval is not without its own in-finite opening:

> At One Hundred and Fifteen Central, we said,
> jokingly, to each other: *Mehr Licht!*, and I insisted
> on translating:
> too much light, even when the ground shook.
> So time, in its underhand way, came apart,
> into this abyss into which nobody ever can see to
> the bottom, as
> you are the first to know, and this end
> which never ends, and which it is necessary to
> perpetuate
>
> still a little, very little, just as is allowed to us. (P, 92–93)

Was the enjoined perpetuation anything other than what Lacoue-Labarthe also felt was granted to him with the experience of his "light existence" in his encounter with the *passante* of the second section, where he wrote, immediately after his account of that exchanged look, what are perhaps the most astonishing lines of this text?

> It is a great thing to have the right
> To go, simply, to go—in nearest proximity, not far.
> (P, 87)

Surely Bailly is correct in declaring that what Lacoue-Labarthe glimpsed here could be only furtive for him: the purest passing of an end that was both disappearance and an opening—a pure deliverance to the day.[67] And with it came, perhaps, *the late return* (known only to one with grey hair) of what was known by the child of Phrase IV, section 3 ("Let us pass over to the other bank")—a child intimate with the immemorial of infancy and already welcoming the coming day. The end I have tried to describe in these last pages was indeed furtive, but did it not achieve, by *spanning* birth and death (in both the survival of infancy and the survival of death—two passages over water), at least the *perpetuation* of that phrase of which Lacoue-Labarthe had spoken in Phrase II, just before introducing the "history of renunciation"? ("At *the limit, that is to say, at those moments of terrifying forgetting when the slightest winter's light on a wall, the poor grass of a garden, the water of a stream is, in hiatus, the pure sign that I'm going to die, I could say, and this too would be pronounced, in silence, would let itself be taken into the phrase: I will have been a phrase*.") Had he not succeeded in *drawing it out* with these last steps at the threshold? *Phrase* will have been for him a kind of rhythmic perpetuation or extenuation, in rare prosody, of the fragmented line.

though it is ephemeral, this, and though
In our night we should not even know
The lines that destiny has fixed for our run.[68]

NOTES

1. Maurice Blanchot, *L'écriture du désastre*, (Paris: Éditions Galilée, 1980). The narrative appears in an English translation by Anne Smock in *The Writing of the Disaster* (Lincoln: University of Nebraska Press, 1986), 72. This text also forms the core of my own meditation on "the death of the *infans*" in *Infant Figures*. Here, as with other citations, I have made slight alterations in the translation. These

are not meant as *corrections* to the valuable work of the translators, but rather reflect my experience with the texts and my relation to them.

2. *The Writing of the Disaster*, 67.

3. *The Writing of the Disaster*, 71.

4. This section, "*L'émoi*," bears the dedication "*à Blanchot*" (the form used also in the other dedications, to Jean-Christophe Bailly and Jean-Luc Nancy, for example). Since this section of *Phrase* foregrounds the question of whether or not what it recounts is a *scene*, the locution takes on a particular intonation (following the French expression *faire une scène à*). It is difficult to attribute such an intention to Lacoue-Labarthe's phrasing with any certainty but it happens that Lacoue-Labarthe drew on the locution to which I have referred for his book on Wagner, *Musica Ficta (figures de Wagner)* (Paris: Christian Bourgois Éditeur, 1991). The first sentence reads as follows in the French: "*Quatre 'scènes' composent ce livre, toutes quatre faites à Wagner* . . ." (11).

I should note that the sections of *Phrase* are dated from 1976 to 2000. But Lacoue-Labarthe had already published literary works that are not without a Blanchotian accent in *Le nouveau commerce* (see *L'"Allégorie"* [Paris: Éditions Galilée, 2011]), and it is not inconceivable that Blanchot had his correspondent's work in view.

5. This volume, edited by Aristide Bianchi and Leonid Kharlamov (Paris: Éditions Galilée, 2011) reprints the section of *Phrase* ("*L'émoi*") to which I have just referred. It contains essays on Blanchot's last published narrative, *L'instant de ma mort* (presented with a facing English translation by Elizabeth Rottenberg in *The Instant of My Death* [Stanford: Stanford University Press, 2000]), as well as a relatively brief treatment of the text by Blanchot from which I started, the "primal scene" Blanchot had sent to Lacoue-Labarthe and Benezet for publication in 1976. This posthumous volume contains many valuable pages, but is somewhat uneven and cannot suffice to convey the true depth of Lacoue-Labarthe's engagement with Blanchot's text and thought, even if it contains an explicit statement by Lacoue-Labarthe on this subject and a contribution on the topic of Blanchot's pre- and post-war politics. Only "*L'émoi*" really shows us the character of this involvement in its literary, philosophical, and genuinely *existential*

senses. I will return to Lacoue-Labarthe's statement on his relation to Blanchot below.

6. *The Writing of the Disaster*, 116.

7. I describe this movement back toward a notion of writing or "archi-writing" (characteristic of deconstruction as Derrida formulated and practiced it in his earlier work, and as Lacoue-Labarthe understood it) in *The Claim of Language: A Case for the Humanities* (Minneapolis: University of Minnesota Press, 2000), 80–81.

8. "The Echo of the Subject" begins with references to two declarations concerning rhythm (from Hölderlin and Mallarmé) that Lacoue-Labarthe finds haunting, but ultimately obscure: beyond his "capacity" and engaging something that one "knows" only as a kind of vague intuition. Mallarmé's phrase is perhaps most immediately pertinent for us: "because every soul is a rhythmic knot" (*Typography*, ed. Christopher Fynsk [Cambridge, MA: Harvard University Press, 1989], 140). "The Echo of the Subject" then goes on to read a section of Theodor Reik's *The Haunting Melody* (the third section, the only one translated into French) in an effort to account for Reik's own "failure" to think through the "catacoustic" phenomenon named in the essay's title. The essay is dense and allusive, counterbalancing the initial modest statements with a concerted display of theoretical sophistication that passes principally by way of Lacan (a crucial reference for Lacoue-Labarthe in this period of his work, particularly as concerns that problem of identification). The intricacies of this analysis need not delay us here, however instructive and interesting they might be. It should be observed, however, that they implicitly pose a profound question to Lacoue-Labarthe's own "autobiographical" gesture in *Phrase*. For, if every autobiography is in fact an allo-biography that is of necessity marked by some agonistic relation with another, thus finally an allo-thanatography (Lacoue-Labarthe presents this as a thesis with general import, but illustrates it with the self-presented case of Reik, wherein the rivalrous conflict centered principally, but not exclusively, on Reik's teacher, Abraham, whose death occasioned the autobiographical and auto-analytic effort undertaken in *The Haunting Melody*), then we can hardly fail to be struck by the position this theoretical articulation prescribes for Blanchot in *Phrase*. To give some

hint of the position Blanchot occupied for Lacoue-Labarthe in this respect, we might consider these words from the late text, "*L'Agonie de la religion*" in *Agonie terminée, agonie interminable*: "So it was when I first heard this voice for the first time forty years ago, deafened, which is to say, still *infans*. Like everyone else, I thought in terms of a vocation" (128). What must one do with a predecessor with this kind of silencing effect if one is destined to writing—at least until that time when one grasps the finitude of that voice? Lacoue-Labarthe continues in "*L'Agonie*": "I didn't perceive that this voice was already expiring, nor that it was growing distant, already, in the murmur in which the brilliance of what it had proclaimed would be veiled." Learning to write about Blanchot, as I came to understand for myself, meant learning that last lesson and thus learning to write from the opening of community that sounded there.

But most immediately pertinent for our current discussion is Lacoue-Labarthe's effort to tie together three elements in Reik's exposition: (1) his attempt to account for the grounds of an autobiographical compulsion ("the necessary re-citation, though deluded and vain in its desire for recognition, of an inaccessible prescription" [264]); (2) his attempt to understand those identifying traits of a "character" that appear in the gesture, the grain of the voice, etc. (which would lead back to "the incised and engraved (or the pre-inscribed), the program of a subject . . . the unconscious as a system of traces, marks, imprints" [251]); and (3) the grounds of possibility of a musical catharsis (275ff.) which, as the opening of the essay suggests, are ultimately rhythmic and thus again point to a form of schematism/writing. The thinking that informs *Phrase* very clearly proceeds from this effort. We might even suggest, on the basis of this essay, that Lacoue-Labarthe had theorized his own auto-thano-tography in advance—even to the point of recognizing that his own effort would require something like the "letting go" or the "renunciation of renunciation" of which Reik proved incapable.

9. In the "Notice" to his book *Heidegger: La politique du poème* (Paris: Éditions Galilée, 2002), Lacoue-Labarthe makes this point in a particularly pained manner. "That part of my activity that one might consider "philosophical," he observes in a parenthesis, will have

always been concerned with him" (11). The cautious and restricted application of the word "philosophy" is echoed in other statements from Lacoue-Labarthe's last fifteen years of intellectual activity (i.e., after the collapse that began to occur in Lacoue-Labarthe's intellectual projects from the time of the composition of *The Fiction of the Political*, which Lacoue-Labarthe names as the predecessor for the questioning pursued in *The Politics of the Poem*). But I believe it is important to take these statements with a measure of reserve. If these statements of philosophical "desistance" are taken too literally (as some have done) the result is a kind of effacement of a vast portion of Lacoue-Labarthe's important work. I think of the work on Plato, Nietzsche, Lacan, and Hölderlin, among others. Of course, one can accept Lacoue-Labarthe's judgment to some degree (but only to some degree) if one restricts the term "philosophy" in the way I did "theory" above—something of this usage may be at work in the words I have cited. Jean-Christophe Bailly pursues considerations of this kind, following suggestions from André Hirt, in a very thoughtful and precise way in *La véridiction* (Paris: Christian Bourgois Éditeur, 2011), applying the same considerations to a term such as "poet," which Lacoue-Labarthe also abjured. But I believe Lacoue-Labarthe is using the word here in the broader sense of a critical practice involved in engaging—in some measure *thinking*—the history of philosophy and its founding concepts. Heidegger had certainly enabled Lacoue-Labarthe in this respect (with others: Granel, Derrida); but his thought was not essentially limited by this reference.

For my purpose here, the crucial point is that Lacoue-Labarthe had taken to heart the impetus Heidegger had identified in the existential analytic (what Heidegger had designated as the first step in "fundamental ontology") as well as the limit it indicated for "philosophical" conceptualizing. "Finitude" named both, and Lacoue-Labarthe was fully aware that this name for the abyssal foundation of the human Dasein retained its force for Heidegger's later thinking.

10. This searing event is recounted in Phrase XVIII, "*(La malediction)*." I will refrain from speculating on Lacoue-Labarthe's relation to his parents in this study, treating only what Lacoue-Labarthe gives us of a maternal figure known in infancy. But it is clear that Lacoue-

Labarthe's own childhood must have been deeply marked by the affects that are painfully recorded in this section of *Phrase*. Here is a truly terrible instance of what Lyotard termed a destructive parental *main-mise*. For this last topic, see Lyotard's volume *Misère de la philosophie* (Paris: Galilée), 117–132.

11. There are, as one might well anticipate, significant precedents for the thinking pursued here by Lacoue-Labarthe. One, in particular, seems especially pertinent in light of the remarks by Lacoue-Labarthe on Malraux in *Agonie terminée, agonie interminable*: "From the time of my years at the *lycée* and the awakening of my first literary passion (this was, in fact, Malraux) . . ." (79). I cite Jean-François Lyotard's *Signé Malraux* (Paris: Grasset, 1996): "Stripped of the authority conferred upon it by a common faith in God or in Man, literary writing sustains itself with what Malraux . . . commenting on *Les nouvelles nourritures* will name a 'particular obsession': a barely conscious matrix upon which the impressions and expressions of a writer obstinately mould themselves and which gives his writing its secret singularity" (241).

12. There is a fateful character to "phrase," as I have noted, and it comes via a language that is ultimately never one's own, even as one takes it over as native. But in the learning of that language, from the earliest babblings, there is also a coming to language of phrase for the subject appropriating it (and disappropriated by it). Phrase is first "phrased" in infancy, as Lacoue-Labarthe recognized already in Phrase II ("*I think of the always innate (degenerated) birth / of* literature: *the diction of children; the prosody older than our memory / of legends*" [P, 17]), and as his argument in *Le chant des muses* (Paris: Bayard, 2005), to which I will return, indicates more fully. There is a fateful reception in this phrasing, but the fact of phrasing makes this destining a singular one.

13. Of course, the other in this relationship necessarily has her own line of experience, which will not go without some characterization in the narrative. But the composition of this text—and this is partly why I will hold to the term "autobiography," despite all the pressure to which Lacoue-Labarthe subjected it—is such that the two lines of Lacoue-Labarthe's own experience receive the determining accent.

14. My work on Blanchot's late, "exilic" writings in *Last Steps* (Fordham University Press, 2013), and specifically his treatment of the questions of friendship and community, has prompted me to use this locution "dying-with" to denote an essential part of what we might understand as the "being-with" that Heidegger claimed was constitutive of the Dasein.

15. The subsequent evocation of Beethoven is found in Phrase XIV, 89–91, one of the most imposing poetic pieces in Lacoue-Labarthe's volume (translated by Leslie Hill in *On Jean-Luc Nancy: The Sense of Philosophy*, ed. Simon Sparks, Darren Sheppard, and Colin Thomas [London: Routledge, 1997], 2–11). Jean-Christophe Bailly offers a superb commentary on what Lacoue-Labarthe draws from Beethoven in *La véridiction*, 72–77. But I should perhaps note that the "fall and closing" of phrase, as it is described here, might also evoke that phrase upon which turns Mallarmé's "*Le démon de l'analogie*," an exquisite prose-poem that begins with the question, "Do unknown words sing upon your lips, cursed shards of an absurd phrase?" There are many lines to cite from this text, beginning with those that present the fall and closing of the phrase in question: "I left my apartment with the sensation that belongs to a wing sliding over the strings of an instrument, light and lingering, replaced by a voice pronouncing the words with a descending tone: '*La Pénultième est morte*' in such a way that *La Pénultième* ends the verse and '*Est morte*' detached itself from the fateful suspension more uselessly in the void of signification." (Stéphane Mallarmé, *Oeuvres complètes* [Paris: Gallimard, 1945], 272–73. Lacoue-Labarthe adopts a very different style from this Mallarméan one in *Phrase*, but it is striking how insistently the term "demon" (now inflected with a thought of the *daimon*) comes back in the essay on Blanchot dedicated to Derrida in *Agonie terminée, agonie interminable*, "*Fidélités*," 63–90.

16. I repatriate once again a term proposed by Jacques Derrida for Lacoue-Labarthe's earlier, and perhaps most important, meditations on the (de)constitution of the subject. Derrida's essay, itself entitled "Desistance," and which I had the honor of translating, forms the introduction for *Typography: Mimesis, Philosophy, Politics*. I might add that I offered for *désistance*, in passing (in playful response to Derrida's

claim that this word could not be re-translated into English), "standing down," which works rather well in relation to the theme of renunciation. See, in particular, p. 4.

17. There is a coy play of identification and reference throughout the volume that I have already noted in the play with "you" and "us" in the verses of the first page. It appears also in the dedication: "For whom other than you?"—a question whose ambiguity inheres in the fact that it might be something other than rhetorical (exposing the *toi* to an *autre*). We touch here on a play of revelation and reserve that marks the narrative as a whole, but also a disruption in reference that follows from the effacement of the subject that occurs in desistance (both as lived and as written).

18. Jean-Christophe Bailly develops this theme beautifully in *La véridiction*. Let me state here that I find this book particularly touching by reason of the manifest friendship that animates it, and for its own distinctive phrasing. It is especially strong in light of the thinking about language that informs it. But Bailly does not follow Lacoue-Labarthe into some of the darker aspects of the thought of phrase, perhaps by reason of constraints relating to this same friendship.

19. The relation between phrase and the notes of supplication, lamentation, etc., that sound throughout the book is difficult to describe conceptually, for reasons that will be clear from what I have said about the "quasi-transcendental" character of phrase. But I believe that my suggestion about the way it sounds in prayer (always in a kind of withdrawal or echo) also finds support in Lacoue-Labarthe's remarks on his understanding of poetic experience in *La poésie comme expérience* (Paris: Christian Bourgois Éditeur, 1986): "A poem has nothing to recount, or even to say: what it recounts and says is that from which it tears itself away as a poem. If one speaks of 'poetic emotion,' one must understand this as *émoi*, which means: an absence or privation of means. 'A *une passante*' is not a nostalgic story of an encounter, but an imploring that arises from a collapse, the pure echo of [such an overwhelming] emotion [*émoi*]: song or prayer" (33).

20. See, for example, Hölderlin's epigram, "Sophocles": "Many have tried, but in vain, with joy to express the most joyful / Here finally it expresses itself to me, here in mourning [*hier in der Trauer*]." In

Friedrich Hölderlin, *Poems and Fragments*, trans. Michael Hamburger (Cambridge: Cambridge University Press, 1980), 72.

21. The term I translate here as "ebbing" is *reflux*, which also appears in a striking manner in Lacoue-Labarthe's essay, "La scène est primitive": "We never apprehend anything more than the *ebb* of death" ("The Scene is Primal," trans. Karen McPherson in *The Subject of Philosophy*, ed. Thomas Trezise [Minneapolis: University of Minnesota Press, 1993], 112).

22. Lacoue-Labarthe's translation of these paragraphs departs in some measure from that offered in the *Pléiade Oeuvres*, ed. Philippe Jaccottet (Paris: Gallimard, 1967), 958. I have tried to stay close to his translation on this occasion, thus producing something quite different from the English translation by Thomas Pfau (in *Friedrich Hölderlin: Essays and Letters on Theory* (Albany: SUNY Press, 1988), 108.

23. In fact, "caesura," as introducing an experience of time, could conceivably apply to the first tracing of that "line" of existence that takes form from the first deliverance to the day, that immemorial birth where phrase itself has *taken* in an individual existence (without ever quite forming). I am inclined to limit the application of the term in this context, however, to the onset of the relation for the fact that Lacoue-Labarthe sees a "truth" emerging there (a crucial point to which we will return).

"Caesura" is used by Hölderlin in a technical sense for the description of tragic structure, but he locates it in both *Antigone* and *Oedipus the King* with the interventions of Tiresias; this "pure word" thus bears a relation to divine powers. Lacoue-Labarthe uses the term without reference to the divine, and it perhaps even says for him a decisive interruption in the possibility of such a reference. It marks for him a breach in the possibility of holy names (I allude here to a text by Heidegger that Lacoue-Labarthe translated: *Der Fehl heiliger Namen: Le défaut des noms sacrés* [Paris: Gramma, 1981]).

24. A long footnote on *Erfahrung* is provided in *La poésie comme expérience*, p. 30. It draws from an article by Roger Munier inspired by Heidegger: "*Experience* comes from the Latin *experire*, to undergo. The radical is *periri*, which is found in *periculum*, peril, danger. The Indo-European root is PER, to which are attached the idea of

traversal, and secondarily that of *épreuve* [a trial or experience undergone]."

25. I am calling here upon a point pursued by Blanchot in the passage cited earlier when he tells us that "the possibility of speech and life would depend, through death and murder, on the relation of singularity established fictively with a mute past, to the hither side of history, thus outside the past, for which the eternal infans becomes a figure, even as it slips away from it." But in drawing upon this passage as I do, I offer an interpretation that diverges quite significantly from what Lacoue-Labarthe presumably made of it, judging from remarks in *Agonie terminée, agonie interminable*. In those remarks, Lacoue-Labarthe claims that Blanchot's discussion of Leclaire and Winnicott in the pages of *The Writing of the Disaster* preceding the appearance of "(A primal scene?)" carry a kind of indictment of the "natural" fictive inclination to which the two analysts have recourse with figures such as the "marvelous (terrifying) child," which takes form in us on the basis of the dreams and desires of those who brought us to the world. Such therapeutic elaborations, which allow some purchase on "the impossible necessary death," are to be grouped, he notes, among products of the *work* of negation or the interiorizing movement of thought. This leads Lacoue-Labarthe to the following conclusion: "But we see immediately what this means: fiction ["*la fiction*," reads the sentence, and thus the reference could be to the particular instance of fictioning in question; but the sentences to follow indicate a broader reference] has no other origin—or any other function—than conceptual or therapeutic, philosophical or analytic *work*. It derives, in the same manner, from the negativity 'at work.' A same logic *organizes* literature, philosophy, and psychoanalysis. It is *logic* itself" (145).

This statement may not be quite as reductive as it sounds (depending on how strictly Lacoue-Labarthe is using his terms), but it is hard to bring it into alignment with Blanchot's own introductory development of the question posed in the opening "Note" of *The Infinite Conversation* (trans. Susan Hanson [Minneapolis: University of Minnesota Press, 1993], xi–xii): "What is at stake for the fact that something like literature should exist?" In any case, it does not seem adequate to the entirety of the discussion in *The Writing of the Disaster*.

Lacoue-Labarthe's remarks focus, in fact, on the first several pages of the long theoretical discussion preceding the appearance of "(A primal scene?)" and do not address the section that appears immediately before it (where we find the sentence I cited at the outset of this note). This section restates the material from the preceding pages, though now under a kind of title (which is Leclaire's title phrase: "a child is being killed"), and reasserts the *necessity* of the "relation of singularity that would be established fictively" for speech and life. One may in fact read the movement of this section as involving a kind of "effacement" of the figure that cannot hold the relation in question (the past outside the past slips away); Leclaire's phrase itself suffers a kind of fragmentation in its manner of "divulging" the "operation" (Blanchot would have heard the reference to "work" in this term), which is nothing other than "the very time that destroys (effaces) time." The movement of this section is in fact quite characteristic of Blanchot's later writing. But the exigency of the figure has clearly been marked, no less than the exigency of writing. And we cannot then ignore the manner in which this account of effacement then cedes to the presentation of "(A primal scene?)." Undoubtedly, Blanchot wants us to read this fragment *in the neutral*, or against the effacement he has just described, but one is still left then with the question of the status of this insistent "fiction." Lacoue-Labarthe makes hesitant steps at the end of his essay to address this question, but I do not believe they begin to account for the text's singular form and figural force, and I do not believe we can accept that Blanchot retained (reprinted) this text in revised form only to the end of "demythologizing" it. His own questioning treatment of it at the end of *The Writing of the Disaster* suggests something quite different.

The provenance of Lacoue-Labarthe's critical rigor in this instance is undoubtedly his struggle with the question of figuration in Heidegger—a subject to which I will have to return in a forthcoming treatment of "The Origin of the Work of Art." But I would note in this context that Lacoue-Labarthe's strictures would seem to have a very unfortunate implication for his own fictive elaborations in *Phrase*.

26. I cannot but suspect that this example may offer something of Lacoue-Labarthe's understanding of the enigmatic phrase that so gripped Bataille in his meditation on the inner experience: "*l'autorité*

s'expie" (a phrase that appears to have been brought to Bataille by Blanchot). Lacoue-Labarthe himself takes up this phrase in *Agonie terminée, agonie interminable*, 128 and 146.

27. Twice this path, this border, is named in *Phrase* (the geographical reference is quite clear). The second, less direct reference appears in Phrase XI (P, 77). Here, Lacoue-Labarthe evokes a fear with respect to a "memory without mention."

28. "And as / often, too, I have thought I heard /in certain voices, poor, exhausted, a kind / of prayer. And perhaps / there is never accorded to us, otherwise / response to that for which / we no longer have a name" (P, 36–37).

29. "If our childhood fascinates us, this happens because childhood is the moment of fascination, itself fascinated." See "The Essential Solitude," in Maurice Blanchot, *The Space of Literature*, trans. Ann Smock (Lincoln: University of Nebraska Press, 1982), 33.

30. "Of childhood, of innocence we have no concept." From *Hyperion, or The Hermit in Greece, Hyperion and Selected Poems*, ed. Eric L. Santner (New York: Continuum, 1990), 4.

31. This is a phrase that preoccupied Lacoue-Labarthe throughout his work (a point to which I can attest even more firmly from personal experience than from textual evidence). But one might consider the text dating from 1992 collected in *Heidegger: La politique du poème* (Paris: Éditions Galilée, 2002), 79–115, "*Il faut*." Reading this phrase in Hölderlin via a discussion of Heidegger, Benjamin, and Adorno, Lacoue-Labarthe argues that the syntagm carries a "demythologizing" force. Needless to say, its impact on the preceding lines from this section of *Phrase* is profound if one allows it all its Hölderlinian resonance and what it implies of a form of sobriety. The essay in question pursues quite thoroughly a number of the key terms introduced in *Phrase* to think what Lacoue-Labarthe sought in a "just prose." We read there, for example, in a quite focused discussion of word-choice in Hölderlin's "Andenken" of "*le renoncement le plus précis*" (which can mean "the most precise renunciation," as well as "in the most precise sense of the term renunciation") by which Hölderlin pursues a form of "de-figuration" or withdrawal from what Lacoue-Labarthe attempts to think with the term "figural."

32. I refer to the concluding page of Blanchot's narrative, translated by Lydia Davis and collected in *The Station Hill Blanchot Reader*, ed. Georges Quasha (Barrytown: Station Hill Press, 1999), 129–88.

33. The exact nature of this judgment, this teaching, remains, however, somewhat obscure at this point in the text. Clearly, it contradicts the affirmative promise of Phrase IV, even as it follows the terms set out there (fear is said to come from the return of the void in us, and thus comes with a kind of dying). But for her, his stricken speaking (bringing to her a silence in their dying-with) clearly fails with regard to the declared promise of that preceding section.

34. In this respect, it is an almost immediate saying of phrase, and very near to what Lacoue-Labarthe named more generally "supplication" in Phrase II. I recall that "phrase" was described as running beneath the modulations of this supplication, which were given with a series of rather extreme examples: "Imagine the body bent over the 'it's nothing' of suffering or the 'why?' without answer of affliction; imagine it failing, its breath caught, but speaking—murmuring. This is supplication. [. . .] There remains—the precarious itself: the few words that pass the throat" (P, 16).

35. Lacoue-Labarthe indicates that what draws him to this word is the reference to death; the *kère* is a goddess "of death itself," in other words, consummate immortality. For a rich scholarly account of the sense of this term in ancient Greek texts, see Jean-Pierre Vernant, "Figures féminines de la mort en Grèce," in *Oeuvres*, Tome II (Paris: Éditions du Seuil, 2007), 1396–412. I thank Michael Eng for this reference.

36. It is striking how the valence of this statement varies from its earlier formulations. Here the figure who announces it comes onto what is apparently a stage, initially hesitating, but proceeding to declare this knowledge decisively: "what we hold to be immemorial (to be born, to die; or, more precisely: to die, to be born) is simply unforgettable. It is the unforgettable itself" (P, 53). The knowledge comes, in other words, almost as something sentenced.

37. There are several references to Hölderlin in these lines. Lacoue-Labarthe will return to one of them in *La poésie comme expéri-*

ence, p. 35, though he gives the phrase in question in a slightly different form ("Nothing is happening to me, nothing is happening to me"). With the emphasis on "nothing" given by Lacoue-Labarthe, in accordance with what he names "poetic existence" ("if existence is what, at moments, tears a hole in life, casting us outside ourselves" [34]), the line would be appropriately translated in this case as "It's nothing, it's nothing."

38. Without long citations, it is impossible to convey the extremity of the lines to which I have referred (one must also follow the passage from section 1, written in the first person, into section 2, written in the third person). I am rather puzzled that these have not received more attention from Lacoue-Labarthe's readers, but at the same time not puzzled, given how raw they are, and unsettling.

39. Lacoue-Labarthe's citation undoubtedly points to Mozart's Requiem, which draws from the thirteenth-century Latin hymn by Thomas of Celano, "Dies Irae," used in the Roman Catholic Requiem mass. The English translation of Mozart's text gives: "When the judge takes his place / What is hidden will be revealed / Nothing will remain unavenged."

40. Lacoue-Labarthe's reserve surely merits the discretion for which it calls, no matter what one thinks one might know from other sources or personal experiences. (How many times did I myself accompany the dogs, Lucrèce and Sappho, down that path?) Let me reiterate that I seek to read the "truth" of a text of prose poetry—i.e., what this text tries to communicate of its own experience with truth, not what is revealed or masked of an autobiography. Personal knowledge cannot be entirely suspended in such a hermeneutic task, but its pertinence must be vigilantly overseen; even in the knowledge that no measure is ever given for this impossible propriety.

41. These words were translated by Lacoue-Labarthe for the production of Hölderlin's translation at the Théâtre National de Strasbourg. See *L'Antigone de Sophocle* (Paris: Christian Bourgois Éditeur, 1978). For this citation, I have translated his translation, p. 59. It is interesting to note that Hölderlin had also cited these lines in his essay, "On Religion" (see *Friedrich Hölderlin: Essays and Letters on Theory*, trans. and ed. Thomas Pfau [Albany: SUNY Press, 1988], 91).

42. Though there is no word of this in his reading of the text in *Agonie* beyond an important reference to a movement beyond the grip of a political trap (the trap of "politics" itself in the form of an ideological war that structured, Lacoue-Labarthe argues, a significant part of French intellectual life through much of the twentieth century [109–22]).

43. The composition of this section (it is dated 1990–2000) spans ten years, but the date of its conclusion coincides with that of the account of the time in the clinic.

44. The admission is followed by the words, "I have nothing to deny"—suggesting there is no reason to withhold at this point.

45. I take up these terms in a reading of Heidegger's explication of George's reference to poetic renunciation in his essay, "The Essence of Language" in *Language and Relation: . . . that there is language* (Stanford: Stanford University Press, 1996), 46–47.

46. I refer, in particular, to *La fiction du politique*. *La politique du poème*, as I have noted, opens with a statement regarding the pain occasioned by a "schizophrenic" relation to Heidegger, a wound to an admiration that remained intact.

47. This conflict was expressed beautifully in the "*quand même*" he used, almost despite himself, in the presence of something whose force or authority he could not but acknowledge. Bailly fondly recalls this in speaking of Lacoue-Labarthe's reaction to the burial mounds in Kyongju, Korea in *La véridiction*, 28.

48. In this very moving statement, Lacoue-Labarthe explains how Blanchot's voice, when he first heard it, seemed to articulate the point of convergence between two "religions" that sought to occupy the vacant place of the theological-political in modernity:

> Everything destined Blanchot to occupy this point of convergence. Like so many others in this century, and in truth almost all of them. But he was . . . Literature itself. His voice—his voice alone, reduced to itself—was Authority. It taught the Myth, in its most cruel truth: that one had to die for the work of language. Deafened, that is to say, still *infans*, this is how, forty years ago, I heard him for the first

> time. I thought, like everyone else, in terms of a vocation. I entertained the hope for a community. I did not perceive that this voice was already expiring, that it was receding, already, into the murmur in which the brilliance of what it had proclaimed would be veiled.

There follows a superb statement on the famous phrase shared by Blanchot and Bataille, "authority expiates itself," in which Lacoue-Labarthe comments on this recession, this "step not beyond" and the task, the exigency that opened from it (*Agonie terminée, agonie interminable*, 127–29).

49. This narrative is without title in *The Infinite Conversation*, trans. Susan Hanson (Minneapolis: University of Minnesota Press, 1993), xiii-xxiii, and without mention in the table of contents. Its initial publication, however, bore the title "The Infinite Conversation." I offer a reading of this text in *Last Steps*, 76–108.

50. From Blanchot's essay "Friendship," in the volume by that name: *L'amitié* (Paris: Gallimard, 1971), 326.

51. I cannot help but express regret regarding Lacoue-Labarthe's difficulty in following Blanchot in this respect, and my sense that he somehow did not have the time he needed. But I touch here upon a motif that would require extensive development, and at this point I can do little more than point to the argument of *Last Steps*, in which I seek to trace the "delivering" to which I refer.

I will note, however, that in his later work Lacoue-Labarthe came to understand the step or "transport" in question as an opening onto a desired innocence that he also attributed to infancy. This view appears in his interpretation of the "deliverance" Blanchot claimed to have experienced at that moment when he faced a firing squad (presented in *The Instant of My Death*). We thus read the following in his analysis of Blanchot's experience:

> It is therefore a question, if we deliver deliverance from its meta-physical or eschatological overlay (liberation from this world), if we abstain from dreamily finding in death the hope of a *survival*—and I'm forgetting nothing of what

> you [Derrida] have written on this subject, and precisely with respect to Blanchot—it is a question, therefore, of an innocence, like that which is credited, and not in any way by chance, to *in-fantia* ('as innocent as the child who has just been born'), that happy state before language. I would say on this occasion: before the *muthos*. The ultimate *nekuia* given to us to read here—but I know that it is illegible without recalling 'A primal scene' ['Suppose, suppose him: the child'], I'll come back to this, I will have to—says perhaps nothing other than this hope for in-nocence (an entirely different hope from that of survival) and offers perhaps nothing other, at the edge of silence, than the discreet effacement of myth. That is to say of evil. (*Fidelités*, 88–89)

This is an intriguing though hardly unproblematic statement that is too brief and allusive to permit a significant critical response (it contains an odd interpretation of Blanchot's notion of survival and could even be read as contradicting the first "example" of Phrase III). But I will note that Blanchot's experience opens beyond the deliverance Lacoue-Labarthe describes here, for it becomes the ground for what Blanchot will call a "compassion for suffering humanity." There is certainly, in Blanchot's little narrative, an account of deliverance from guilt (which is what Lacoue-Labarthe accents with this emphasis on the infant's "in-nocence"), though it is linked most immediately in the text to class difference and the injustice this allows. But in the light of the massive burden of guilt expressed in *Phrase*, the insistence on this motif ("and not by accident") appears to have a strong personal charge. The only child appearing in *The Instant of My Death* belongs to that *cortège* that returns to the house before the execution in preparation.

The suggestion I make here regarding the limits of Lacoue-Labarthe's reading might be illustrated with respect to his understanding of what Blanchot means when he says that the fading traces left to us in forgetting of "the impossible necessary death" call on one (the writer) to "*except oneself from the cosmic order*" (*The Writing of the Disaster*, 66). Lacoue-Labarthe sees only the appeal to "disaster" in this passage (as we see when he drops this last phrase in re-citing the sentence in which it appears on p. 148 in *Agonie terminée, agonie interminable*) and passes over the question of the conditions of the act of "exception," to which I referred above in evoking a "strange capacity." "Renunciation," as Lacoue-Labarthe develops it, would have been one of those conditions, but does not quite give us the affirmative turn of "exception" in Blanchot's writing and thought.

52. I refer to my preface to *Typography*, x.

53. Lacoue-Labarthe's long-standing sensitivity to this question is visible in the volume he co-edited with Mathieu Benezet: *Haine de la poésie* (Paris: Christian Bourgois Éditeur, 1979). His contribution of the first two "Phrases" to this collection was justified in several respects, but most immediately by the declaration from his "Post-Scriptum": "I detest what is classed under the name of poetry" [in the version published in 2000, *détester* becomes *exècrer*]. On this theme, see also *La poésie comme expérience*.

54. I refer here to Lacoue-Labarthe's amazed and disconcerted discovery in Blanchot's *The Instant of My Death* of what he took to be a citation of Rousseau (citing, in turn, Montaigne's account of a near-death experience after a fall). Quoting Blanchot's concluding reference to the "feeling of lightness which is death itself," he declares, "But this is a citation!" (*Agonie*, 85). The term, one has to presume, is being used in an approximate sense (the connection is not as immediate as Lacoue-Labarthe suggests, and certainly other texts could be marshalled in the context of this evocation of lightness). What is at stake more fundamentally, for Lacoue-Labarthe, is the way Blanchot would be repeating a "fundamental" scene for Western literature, this despite his inexhaustible effort to withdraw from myth. "But the one who will henceforth be called, desperately, 'the last Blanchot,' will have desired ceaselessly to rid himself of that haunting, which is demonic repetition itself—or the eternal resifting of a *re-ligere*" (*Agonie*, 85). The next paragraph begins with the statement that this deliverance cannot be attained, though Lacoue-Labarthe will go on to insist on the exigency involved with an important citation from Blanchot's statement in "Intellectuals in Question" regarding the Jewish renunciation of myth. What is perhaps most moving in this analysis, however, is

Lacoue-Labarthe's struggle with the question of autobiography (vis-à-vis the autobiographical element in Blanchot's narrative) and his own "failure" to resist its insistence. The first paragraph of this essay, addressed to Jacques Derrida, reveals that he is giving in to what a defensive phrase had sought to fend off: "I will not succumb; I don't want the return, the endless return of the same demons . . . ." The ritual repetition of this phrase cannot stem the pronunciation of this other ("just as emphatic"): "I will give in to autobiography, then, I will sacrifice to it (*j'y sacrifierai*)." The latter phrase, he adds, required its public enunciation. It goes without saying that these words reflect on *Phrase* itself, suggesting that the testimonial component may require even more attention than I have given to it. But, as it happens, the reference to sacrifice (and clearly, this too is a word linked to renunciation) has a particular resonance in this address, this letter addressed to Derrida. Not only was sacrifice (as the motif is pursued in Bataille, particularly in his article "Hegel, Death, and Sacrifice") the topic of Lacoue-Labarthe's seminar teaching when *The Instant of My Death* reached him (a long citation of a critical passage from Bataille's essay indicates why the question of *scene* remained so urgent for Lacoue-Labarthe). It was also, as Lacoue-Labarthe notes in closing, the motif of a question from Derrida that had clearly shaken him. What drove him back to autobiography had something to do with this traumatic event (I use the term with all due attention, having witnessed the event) from 1987.

55. Well into the "scene," we read the following, which identifies Lacoue-Labarthe with a gentle self-irony: "He, the aged child, checks the stability of the table, puts the chair in place, and sits down. He arranges the sheets before him with care. He holds his forehead with his two hands, a gesture that seems familiar for him. He remains silent" (P, 102). The staging of this "scene" in Phrase XVII (a veritable aging in citation) was anticipated by a publication from 1979 which presents a series of nine photographic portraits of Urs Lüthi undergoing a process of aging (these are portraits in a classical form that employ makeup, lighting, and pose to achieve their successive effect). This study entails one of Lacoue-Labarthe's most sustained reflections on the question of mimesis, and offers something of a glimpse of his read-

ing of Blanchot. It is also a somewhat unsettling piece in that the photographic portraits of Lüthi call strongly to mind Lacoue-Labarthe himself; one gets the impression that he looked into the mirror to see a painted likeness (as Hölderlin put it) in the form of a dandy. *Portrait de l'artiste en général* (Paris: Christian Bourgois Éditeur, 1979).

56. See, for example, "*La naissance est la mort*" in *Agonie terminée, agonie interminable*, 119–25. The two "primal scenes" involve anger (the text I have cited focuses on the anger of Artaud) and an experience of death; Lacoue-Labarthe would cite the second in *La disparition* (Paris: Christian Bourgois Éditeur, 2011) as an experience of the origin of poetry.

57. *Friedrich Hölderlin, Essays and Letters on Theory*, 150. The line is from the letter to Böhlendorff of December 4, 1801.

58. Lacoue-Labarthe once remarked to me that he was quite proud of the fact that his name bore a link to Heidegger's: both evoked in their etymological origins a spring in damp earth or a field ("coue" would be equivalent to "egger," while "barthe" would be equivalent to "heid" or "heide"). I recall this in this context not for the link to Heidegger (which is arresting in itself), but for Lacoue-Labarthe's way of hearing his own name. I thank Claire Nancy for generously confirming this recollection.

"Clarification" probably bears another meaning in Phrase XXI, to which I will return below. It would imply, I believe, the rendering-audible of something barely heard or muffled—here, a "possible" language. But "*clair*," in *Phrase*, is recalled in any appeal to the Latin *clarus* or any evocation of a brilliant transparency.

59. This is, in fact, a relatively rare statement in *Phrase* about the possibility of writing phrase or the separation brought in the relation with the other (again, they are at times "indistinguishable"): "*All of this cannot be said—barely, barely can it be written. (And if this can be written, it requires a decision come from afar, one must wait, undergo this trial of waiting: perhaps only the rhythm of a phrase can bring us to feel a little, can render, such a wrenching.")* (P, 73).

60. I draw, here, upon a translation by Wallace Fowlie, revised by Seth Whidden, available in *Rimbaud: Complete Works, Selected Letters, a Bilingual Edition*, (Chicago: University of Chicago Press, 2005).

61. It is rather striking that Lacoue-Labarthe significantly misdates the "Phrase" in question. *Phrase* gives this date as "(circa 1985–1986)." But Lacoue-Labarthe had already offered this segment in a publication named *Retrait de l'artiste, en deux personnes* (Lyon: Éditions mem/Arte Facts, 1985), 24–26, a text co-authored with François Martin that includes a facing translation into English by Mira Kandar. Lacoue-Labarthe's preface bears the indication, "Les Ayes, le 28 octobre, 1982," but the legal title of the text in fact suggests its own date: *Retrait de l'artiste, en deux personnes (2 février—16 mars 1981)*, and there is no telling when the segment later published in *Phrase* was itself composed, particularly inasmuch as the grounds for its insertion in the volume remain a bit tenuous. It appears suddenly in a kind of diary of Lacoue-Labarthe's efforts to undertake the project to which he agreed with Martin. The error may be, in fact, insignificant, but it could also be that the desire to place it at a later date in *Phrase* answered to the conception of this volume in its final form. Lacoue-Labarthe, I surmise, somehow wanted this segment to come later.

62. This capture may perhaps be linked to what Blanchot termed "fascination" in his meditation on the image in *The Literary Space*. This theme is cited by Lacoue-Labarthe in *Portrait de l'artiste en général*, 85.

63. The phrase comes from "The Echo of the Subject," where it is used as the title for the last section. There, Lacoue-Labarthe describes Reik's brief access to a *rhythmic origin* (which is not properly "musical") for the catacoustic phenomena he is seeking to understand, the "haunting melody." He declares however, that the "maternal closure" is perhaps insuperable, even while asking, "Of what else, other than the mother, could there in fact be reminiscence? What other voice could come back to us? What else could echo, resonate in us, seem familiar to us? Let us recall the 'place where each of us once dwelled,' the 'I know this, I've already been here'—and thus, 'I've already heard it.' Plato thought that mothers are the ones who impose or imprint upon each of us our type. How else, in fact, would we be rhythmed?" (*Typography*, 205–206). A similar theoretical caution marks the speculation on the origin of music in Phrase XVI (P, 97–98), in that the mother is not named, though the thesis of a "resonance of the unheard . . . from before we were thrown / From before even our

immortal effacement" appears to be strengthened. But in *Le chant des muses* (Paris: Bayard, 2005), the "insuperable" limit for theory appears to be ignored. There, as I have noted, Lacoue-Labarthe offers a theory of the origin of music that traces its origins back to "a very deep memory" stemming from a time before birth (the nature and possibility of this memory is not treated) and identifies the affect it produces as the most ancient emotion: joy (26, 37). (Was the fact that he was speaking to a young audience sufficient to allow this lifting of the barrier?) In this context, his definition of clarification is worth noting:

> Luminous transmission is, for our perception, our sensibility, practically instantaneous. The transmission of sound is not. It is therefore necessary to bring aid to it, to *clarify* it. One must give to sound the possibility of crossing a distance that it crosses with difficulty, particularly if it is the distance between the before and the after of birth! [. . .] (I use the word 'clarification' because 'clear'—*clarus* in Latin—is an adjective originally used for the voice, not for colours or light. This designates a voice that is distinct and firm.) We thus obtain the following: music has for its task that of *clarifying* the (maternal) stifling of sound. In the womb of its mother, the child undoubtedly does not distinguish itself from the body of its mother: there is no space, no distance. If it hears, this makes it react immediately: move, undergo a movement, be *moved* (*ému*), in the strong sense of the term. What I mean is that if music exists, this is in order to discover this first, this very first *emotion*. (37–38)

64. Not to mention the "nobility" of the girl encountered on the street in Blanchot's *Le pas au-delà*.

65. For this passage over "*le peu profound ruisseau*" (here, Mallarmé), see the moving final chapter of *La véridiction*, "L'infinitif de la césure" (53–76), where Jean-Christophe Bailly links a reading of Phrase XIV to the brief text Lacoue-Labarthe composed after another return from death (again, double in character, this time over a period

of only a few months in 2006), published in a volume he edited under the title *Préface à la disparition* (Paris: Christian Bourgois Éditeur, 2009), 45.

66. Though Lacoue-Labarthe would have been evoking both the extraordinary music and the speech (as is suggested by *Le chant des muses*, 31). James Blood Ulmer's oeuvre is immense, but to catch something of what Lacoue-Labarthe sought in the music, one might consider *Birthright* (Hyena Records, 2005). It would not be hard to overlay the Hölderlinian scheme of "remembrance" on this section of *Phrase* which recounts exposure to the foreign. Following this thought, but in a slightly different mode, I like to imagine Lacoue-Labarthe listening to James Blood Ulmer's "Are You Glad to be in America?" (*Blood and Burger* [Dernière Bande Musique, 2003]—it is Rodolphe Burger who would have introduced Lacoue-Labarthe to the music of Blood Ulmer).

67. "Everything transpires here as though the 'pure gift of self to relation' of which Benjamin speaks once again in relation to Hölderlin, had forever been eclipsed, as though it had never had the fortune of coinciding with a form: except for the moment of a flash in which the impossible had been possible, where, in other words, the condition [of poetic existence] had become a threshold" *La véridiction*, 71.

68. Pindar, 6th Nemean Ode, following the translation proposed by Philippe Lacoue-Labarthe and Claire Nancy, *Lignes* (Paris: Nouvelles Éditions Lignes, 2007), 247.

INDEX OF NAMES